double
drink story
My Life With
DYLAN THOMAS

caitlin
thomas

with an afterword by
Francesco Fazio

VIKING

VIKING
Published by the Penguin Group
Penguin Books Canada Ltd, 10 Alcorn Avenue, Toronto, Ontario,
Canada M4V 3B2
Penguin Books Ltd, 27 Wrights Lane, London W8 5TZ, England
Viking Penguin, a division of Penguin Books USA Inc., 375 Hudson
Street, New York, New York 10014, U.S.A.
Penguin Books Australia Ltd, Ringwood, Victoria, Australia
Penguin Books (NZ) Ltd, cnr Rosedale and Airborne Roads, Albany,
Auckland 1310, New Zealand

Penguin Books Ltd, Registered Offices: Harmondsworth,
Middlesex, England

First published 1997

1 3 5 7 9 10 8 6 4 2

Printed and bound in the U.S.A.

Canadian Cataloguing in Publication Data

Thomas, Caitlin
Double drink story

ISBN 0-670-87378-0

1. Thomas, Dylan, 1914–1953 – Marriage. 2. Thomas, Caitlin –
Marriage. 3. Poets, Welsh – 20th century – Biography.
4. Authors' spouses – Wales – Biography. I. Title.

PR6039.H52Z86 1997   821'.912   C97-930362-1

Visit Penguin Canada's web site at **www.penguin.ca**

For Giuseppe

who has helped me more than anybody
in my combat against the enemy

"…I stick to what I know personally and never try to emulate others better than myself. Least of all to emulate Dylan. That is the fatal mistake of many people…"

contents

a note from the editor

Caitlin Macnamara was born in Hammersmith, London, on December 8, 1913, the youngest of four children. John was the eldest; Nicolette and Brigit were only one and two years older than Caitlin. Their parents, Francis and Yvonne, supported themselves on modest allowances from their families. Francis, who fancied himself a poet, also pursued a life of free love and free thinking, often away from his family.

Finally after seven years of marriage the couple separated. Shortly afterwards, Yvonne and the children moved to a former pub, called New Inn House, in Blashford, near Ringwood. There, Caitlin and her sisters (John was often away at school and later in the navy) grew up in an unstructured manner with plenty of fresh air and plain food, but little in the way of formal education, except for the occasional French governess sent by Yvonne's family. Among the people who surrounded the family were the artist Augustus John and Gerald and Nora Summers. Nora and Yvonne spent much time together, although Nora didn't live with them. The children hated her, but Yvonne apparently maintained a long affair with her.

Caitlin's first love was Caspar John, son of Augustus, with whom she was totally infatuated for a couple of years, although the relationship remained innocent.

In 1931 Caitlin, together with Augustus John's daughter Vivien, went to London to become a dancer. She had some modest success, although she never attained the glory of her idol, Isadora Duncan. She also became a model for Augustus John, who, as she later said, "pounced" on her, as he did most women. The young blonde dancer and the much-older artist had an affair that lasted on and off for a couple of years. Trips to Dublin and Paris followed, but

Caitlin mostly remained in London.

Her meeting with Dylan Thomas, then a promising poet, took place on April 12, 1936, at the Wheatsheaf in London. The two married a year later on July 11, 1937, living first with his parents and later with Caitlin's mother. In 1938 they moved to Laugharne in Wales, which was to be their base for years to come. Their first house there, which they rented, was called Sea View. After the war, an early patron, Margaret Taylor, wife of the historian A.J.P. Taylor and an old friend of Dylan's, bought a house there called the Boat House, which she lent to Caitlin and Dylan.

The war years brought two children—Llewelyn in 1939 and Aeronwy in 1943—and more success for Dylan, who worked for Strand Films and the BBC and published *The Map of Love* in 1939 and *Portrait of the Artist as a Young Dog* in 1940. In 1949 the third of their children, Colm, was born.

At Laugharne, the couple lived a simple life with a regular routine. In the morning Dylan would go off to see Ivy Williams, who ran Brown's Hotel with her husband, Ebie. In the afternoon he would write, and Caitlin would look after the children and the house, and spend time near the sea. In the evenings Dylan would return to Brown's Hotel and Caitlin would join him later for more drinking. When they were away from Laugharne, the children, especially Llewellyn, were often left in the care of Caitlin's mother or sent off to school. In 1949 Dylan's parents moved to a house nearby.

The postwar years brought more fame to Dylan. He acquired a number of patrons, including Marged Howard-Stepney, and an invitation from John Malcolm Brinnin to lecture in New York, which he did in 1950. There he had an affair with a woman named Pearl, who later visited him in London. Margaret Taylor told Caitlin of the woman's presence, prompting a serious rift in the marriage. Caitlin responded with more drinking bouts and a succession of infidelities—although hers were close to home, and his far away.

The two were reconciled, but when Dylan planned his next trip, Caitlin was torn between her desire to accompany him—to protect him from what she saw as predatory North American women—and her pregnancy. She eventually decided to have an abortion rather than leave her husband on his own. The 1952 trip brought out the most outrageous behaviour in Caitlin. She did not accompany Dylan on his next trip in the spring of 1953, when he had an affair with Liz Reitell, or his final trip in the fall of that year. On November 5 in New York he collapsed. Caitlin was sent for and arrived shortly before his death on November 9. At the hospital where Dylan lay, she had to be restrained in a straitjacket, after which she was briefly institutionalized.

After Dylan's death, Caitlin stayed in England for a troubled period, then left for the island of Elba, which she and Dylan had visited years earlier. There she began work on the pain-racked book *Leftover Life to Kill*. Over the next few years she spent most of her time in Italy, with occasional brief visits to England. The money from Dylan's work provided a meagre living. After a move to Italy in 1957, when she was forty-four, she met Giuseppe Fazio. Eleven years her junior, he worked in films and was seen by her friends as a more appropriate companion for her.

The relationship had its ups and downs over the next years as the couple travelled between England and Italy and separated at least once as a result of Caitlin's alcoholism. Then in 1963, just as her book *Not Quite Posthumous Letter to My Daughter* appeared, Caitlin gave birth to Giuseppe's son, Francesco. She was forty-nine.

Caitlin's many attempts at sobriety were unsuccessful until 1973, when she decided to try Alcoholics Anonymous. There she found support and understanding, and began writing about her experiences.

She lived the rest of her life in Italy, enjoying the outdoor life, the culture and her family. She died in 1994, at the age of eighty-one, and is buried next to Dylan in Laugharne.

introduction

Although many very good biographies have been written about Dylan Thomas, I feel that none of their professional authors, even with the best will in the world and all their brilliance, knows what I know about Dylan and our relationship. I also feel my contribution will provide an interesting sidelight on Dylan's character and life to many less intellectual people like myself. I therefore can but try to add my little personal contributions to the colourful picture.

I think I started feeling better when I stopped thinking that I absolutely *had* to become a great writer, that I absolutely *had* to produce an immortal work. I can't imagine what gave rise to this idea, but it has been my conviction since I can remember. The urge to write persisted despite the fact that there was no reason to suppose that I should ever become a great writer. I had had hardly any education; my father, Francis Macnamara, did not believe in educating girls. He left Oxford, where he was studying law, to become a professional eccentric and an inferior poet who believed in free love. He died an abysmal failure.

To my natural shortcomings as a writer was added, ironically, the biggest disadvantage of all: I was married to a genuinely great writer. As a result, I hardly ever dared to put pen to paper in his lifetime. It was only after Dylan's death that I ran riot and let loose my pent-up feelings in a desperate effort at self-expression. The result, *Leftover Life to Kill*, was inflamed by the gross presumptions that accompany excessive drinking, and it served only to show the extent of my unbridled ignorance and of my ungrammatical desperation. As a literary work, its value was nil; it was no more than a splash in a puddle at a time when the whole world was smarting from Dylan's untimely death. And in due course, after its short-lived sensational value, it faded into the limbo of forgotten things where it rightly belonged. I had things to say but I did not know how to write. It was as simple as that.

However, the sense of being set apart and having a burning mission (a common complaint of alcoholics, I believe) is rather pleasant and hard to let go of. It has served me all my life as a convenient excuse for getting out of doing boring housework and cooking. With the common sense of sobriety, I am no longer pressured by my burning mission. But although it is a relief to be free of it, I must admit that I *do* miss it; I need to feel some other purpose in life beyond being simply sober.

All my prayers (I do say prayers, to whom I don't quite know) say: "Let it not all be for nothing." Meaning there must be something more in life than what I have got. I keep forgetting that, in truth, I have had my life with all its immutable mistakes and that what I have now, with the aid of my husband, Giuseppe, my son Francesco, the Alcoholics Anonymous meetings and my own fighting spirit, is a perfectly undeserved bonus which I must learn to be quiet in, to appreciate and in which to be still.

double drink
story

drink

1

Bulldozing Booze as the Prime
Thought in Our Lives

I first met Dylan, inevitably, in a pub, since pubs were our natural habitat. From that day onwards, we became dedicated to pubs and to each other. Pubs were our primary dedication; each other our secondary. But one fit so snugly into the other that they were perfectly complementary.

Ours was not only a love story, it was a drink story, because without alcohol it would never have got onto its rocking feet. My drink story began, *seriously*, with Dylan. Not that I had never taken a drink before, God forbid! I was never one to refuse anything. Alcohol was something I gulped down— all too willingly no doubt, without thinking about it. I was excessive in everything and despised moderation. So did Dylan, unfortunately. There was a fatal similarity in our half-baked ideas, the incredibly childish notions that we thought were so profound, on how one ought to live—or rather, how *we* ought to live—or, to be more exact, how "the chosen" ought to live.

These convenient, if absurd, theories of ours gave unlimited licence to both of our worst defects of excess. To drink moderately, we were absolutely convinced, was definitely beneath us. Only miserable, frightened little people did that. And we, of course, were automatically up among the bold, unafraid, unruly Greats.

There was never any doubt about this in either of our minds. Not even in mine was a tiny crack of doubt allowed to percolate. Nor was I content to live on borrowed light. Oh no, not a bit of it. That was not good enough for me. It had to be all my shining own.

So we belonged, quite simply, no question about it, to the Greats, whose solemn duty was to surfeit ourselves limitlessly with drink, to wild extinction, only to begin again—after passing out and coming to—with renewed vigour. Again and again, and yet again. It was our way of life from the very beginning.

It was bloody boring a lot of the time, but there was no getting out of it. It was our self-made, romanticized prison of drink. But we didn't know then that we were building our own death cells. We just thought, if we thought at all, that we were being frightfully revolutionary.

There was also a connection between the degradation of drink and the purifying purging process. Through degradation came purification. The lower we got, the higher we got— after, presumably, a decent pause had elapsed. Or, to put it more plainly, we had to wallow in shit in order to soar later on to the peaks. It was all part of that ridiculous romantic myth that said, in effect: not until you have passed through the Gates of Hell, not until you have passed through the blinding baptism of fire, are you fit to be a creator of the genuine burning stuff.

Well, we passed through the Gates of Hell and through the blinding baptism of fire all too often. They were all too familiar byways, those well-trodden routes of ours. But the "genuine burning stuff" was a bit slow in coming. More often it evaporated in the fumes of drink or got choked in the fogs of drink. Or came out in all the wrong ways—in the mad morbid excrescences of drink.

From where, then, and from whom did this sacred drinking ritual come? This command to pour down the filthy poison till we dropped in our tracks? Till we crumpled up—after ten hours or more standing—still valiantly hanging on to the bar? The bar was our altar. No saint's altar was more sacred. It was our first and last thought in the day. First, how to get to the bar; last, how to stay put at the bar. It was our great joint mission in life.

Neither of us ever dreamt of chucking such a foul bedfellow out of our bed. It was he who got us to bed together in the first place. We would never have done it without him, for we were both, to our shame, in sober secret, puritanically inclined. It gradually got, so it seemed, so we could never do anything without him. He had become not only our precious daily companion, but also our indispensable lifeblood. Without him, we were not "in life."

In the sober remains of my mind I can't work out what fixed obsession, what crazy compulsion made us do it so faithfully and with such devotion, such undeviating purpose. We hadn't got, between us, enough money to keep one fish floating, let alone two, but in the drinking world money is almost immaterial. Especially if you are young and winning, with a rare gift of the gab. There are nearly always ways of getting a drink for those with a real will, especially if one is wedded to a big, fat, dripping slice of Welsh cunning. Had we put one fraction of the money and bottled energy we put into drinking into some constructive purpose, we should have been building skyscrapers by now and stewing in our own virtuous juices. Instead, Dylan killed himself with false heroics, trying to make the poet more important than his poetry, selling the poet instead of selling the poetry. And succeeding all too well.

In fact, he made him so important that, like the frog in the fable, he blew himself up till he burst. As pathetic and awful as that. And he left one of us to stew in the wicked juices of his perfectly unnecessary sacrifice—in the name of that confounded poetry.

He should have known better, known that a poet should stay under his poet's toadstool, and not parade his talent in the singeing light—or its petals will wilt and die. As indeed they did.

I never really knew Dylan. I knew only one very limited side of him: the sleeping and drinking side. Which is to say, almost all of the outside touchable side of Dylan, but nothing of the inner untouchable side of him, which was considered in the eyes of the world, of course, the much more important one. I was content with the animations of his body; I wanted none of the entanglements of his shady mind.

Sleeping and drinking together with a person does not mean that you get to know that person through and through. Not even in the mere physical sense, for drink makes the body anonymous too. In fact, I believe that we were complete strangers one to the other.

I was to Dylan what he wanted me to be: a lovely, lovelorn, peasant Irish lass lamenting his departure and awaiting, my heart bursting in my breast, for his return. I did my best to suit him in the peasant part, as my intentions, although obtuse and boneheaded, were true enough. But his romantic image of me was not what I was: it had nothing to do with what I was.

I don't think either of us had the slightest idea of what the other was like inside. We were both so egotistic we never looked at, let alone studied, the other's possibilities. At the same time, each of us was quite happy to tolerate the other's ego, so long as it did not interfere with our own. Even had I tried (which I did not), I could never have understood Dylan's intellectual side. He had the Welsh shrewd sense to keep it carefully concealed from me. Not only from me, but from almost everybody, apart from a few chosen exceptions. I never thought of him as a proper intellectual, all specs and scholarly air, although, with the wordy baggage which he carted from bar to bar in his bulging head, he could hardly escape from being one. I think I thought, as nonsensically as he thought about me, that his gift of poetry had descended from the sky like the Holy Spirit entering into the Virgin Mary.

Dylan and I treasured his gift from heaven like a golden casket, intended for us alone. It was an unwritten law between us never to mention it, in case by doing so we would take away some of its magic. We hid it so effectively that it rarely got a chance to surface. It was officially allowed out freely only when we had retired all tattered and torn from the big wicked city to our distant home-bogs. There the outlook stretched into such eternities of boredom that Dylan, in near desperation, had no alternative but to whip his gift out of its stable and give it its mane-tossing head.

Should there be any scepticism about my allegiance to Dylan's gift, I can but add that not only did I devoutly believe in it, but I would not have even considered accepting to live with him without it. Because, in my honest estimation, without his gift he would not have been worthy of me. It must be remembered that Dylan, in his bodily exterior, was not exactly a glamour boy. Without the excuse of the poetry inside him, it would have been a disgrace to my vanity to go around with or to openly cohabit with such a short (he was hardly an inch taller than me), comical figure. For many years I did not believe that any other woman would find him attractive enough to go to bed with. In my ingenuousness, I did not realize then that women of the world went to bed with promising names, not promising bodies. So I concluded that since Dylan was superior to me in brains and I was superior to him in body, we were just about equal: we complemented each other. But how we could have possibly imagined that we would achieve our ends—he of cultivating his brain in order to become the greatest poet of the age, and I of cultivating my body in order to become the greatest dancer of the age (an even less likely presumption)—by continually drinking in pubs until we fell into a torpor is still an insoluble mystery to me.

All we both wanted at heart was to make our own special kind of music to the best of our abilities. But in retrospect, it would seem that both Dylan and I felt that our primary aim was to show off, to simply get ourselves noticed at any outrageous cost. Whether we were noticed in a good or bad light was immaterial to us. We knew only too well that it is much easier and quicker to get noticed in a bad light. It was essential for Dylan's poetic reputation to give people a legend, which, to be efficacious, had to be monstrous, with (inescapably) a fatal ending. In fact, that was the only area in Dylan's life in which he was known to have kept his word! The traditional thing to do in order to be self-respecting Artists with a capital "A" was to destroy ourselves in the noble name of impersonal creation. To put it in more plebeian terms, we gave ourselves unlimited liberty to be out-and-out bastards. We were the biggest bastards out: we thought of nobody else except ourselves. Other people, "the scum of the earth," were put there solely to help or deter us. And God help the ones who deterred us.

The shaming truth was that we were both so devilishly shy (though we had much too much false pride to ever admit it openly) that we would go to any lengths to disguise it. Dylan and I came to be known, even affectionately, by some kind, naïve people as "The Two Terrible Children." We liked this derogatory appellation. It gave us a pleasing sense of our own importance: we had not worked so hard for nothing. The tiny worm of conscience, which wriggled inside us both, was kept under control by our constantly pressing for more and more shots of firewater like two spoilt and capricious children.

Dylan, to be sure, had the powerful weapon of his winning charm, aided by skilful verbal quipping and melting persuasion, to give the lie to our purely selfish intentions and desires. Then, of course, there was his now-famous sonorous, throbbing, booming voice, which even then he laid on with a shovel. With women, Dylan's special forte in the charm line was to make himself even tinier than he really was, to accentuate his bush of unkempt curls, to make his swimming eyes bulge out even more pathetically, to flaunt the varied collection of moulting rags on his back and to play up unscrupulously his utter dejection, his poverty and pennilessness, his little-boy-lost-with-nowhere-to-go-for-the-night act. He managed to suggest that beneath his melancholic clown exterior was lodged the dissolute genius waiting to be saved by his guardian angel. It was nearly impossible for any maternally inclined woman to resist folding him into her comforting arms, squeezing and cuddling him, and taking him home to keep him warm and fed. Then, inevitably, putting him to bed with her like a lovable, dishevelled, shabby and distinctly grubby teddy bear. Of course the big mistake that these women made was that they believed, as Dylan intended they should, that they were unique, that they were the one and only chosen repository of his cosily glowing heart, beating trustfully beside them, and of his weighty head pressing down into the ample folds of their grateful breasts.

In reality, he had providently positioned his Saving Graces at all the pubs within the boundaries of his pub crawling. There were so many of these thinking-themselves-unique beings that he was almost certain of finding a safe bed and breakfast.

I had a searing jealousy of Dylan's real and imagined infidelities: a jealousy that was like an evil growth in my stomach that I could not vomit up; that tore me apart as a draper tears apart a length of country cloth. First of all, I could not conceive that Dylan would actually dare to betray me physically, let alone that he should want to do so. What happened to all his soft-soaping and buttering-up? What unutterable nerve, shameless gall, to betray our sworn oaths of faithfulness to each other forever! To the bitter end, when there was no longer any question of the reality of his conquests and his treacheries, he still stoutly denied them to me. He blatantly lied that no such malicious calumny could ever, in a thousand years, happen to us Special Two, to our Special Love: surely I knew that! Why, he would never even dream of such an absurd thing! Perhaps he did not even dream of it (there was no time between drinks!), but he still did it. Second, I was furious (and, yes, resentful) at the unfairness of it all: that such a comic, stunted puppet of a man (and my man to boot!) should have unlimited opportunities to pick and choose whomsoever momentarily tickled his fancy. Because of his literary reputation alone, he was positively bombarded by famous glamorous women. My perhaps over-fertile imagination visualized these "blatant thieves of my love" on a vast international canvas, on the immense "emancipated" American canvas, where promiscuity was less significant than partaking of a cup of tea. Meanwhile I was confined to the limited landscape of local oafs. Though I did my level best to keep up with Dylan's outrages, to wreak my vengeance on him, to better him, I could not really pretend that my rustic conquests stood up to his notorious worldly ones. Besides, to make matters worse, Dylan merely shrugged off any reports of my scandalous misdoings as so much malicious gossip. It was impossible for him to associate such cheap scandal-mongering, such obviously made-up envious rot, with his haloed romantic image of me. What his poet's eye did not wish to see, it did not see.

This painful period of my bogged-down life of abandonment and frustration (was it really so very different from any of the other periods of my life with Dylan?) hurts even now when I dwell upon it, but I doubt that I have any conception of how painful it was then. How could I have been brought so low without even being aware of it? I fondly imagined that I was having a whale of a time, doing all the clever enviable things, extravagantly boozing and whoring on a grand scale. I think I pictured myself, in the bad old antiquated style, as a flashing courtesan! Whereby a common whore, when she is rich, gaudy, ostentatious and flamboyant enough, becomes a grand duchess, an accepted, envied and infamously revered member of society, next best thing to an actress, if not better.

It should also be borne in mind that during these trials of amorous prowess (which is precisely what they were, with not a bit of genuine desire in them), drink was always lavishly flowing. It was a point of honour for me to prove—what? Something as childish as the potency of my sexual attraction? More than that, to prove that I was not, when evidently I was, an old maid left on the shelf. I may sound ridiculously silly, but women—and I was a first-class bitch of a woman then— are ridiculously silly. When deeply wounded, they are capable of violent ferocious retaliation. Like a provoked wild animal in a cage, they claw and scratch impotently at the bars. Mind you, I am not saying men have not got vanity—as much or more and as petty—but men are not usually driven to such ignominious lengths to hold their supremacy.

To be brutally frank—if I have not made myself sufficiently clear so far—I never went to bed with a man unless I was drunk. And he had to be in the same condition, or else I could not think of him as a right and proper man. The messy business of the sexual act for me was indissolubly connected with the inflammation of drink. The very thought of it without alcohol was not only inconceivable but positively repulsive. It was a much too embarrassing and ugly thing to tackle stone-cold sober. And so strong is the force of bad habit and misguided conditioning that even today I shudder at the idea of doing such an indecent thing without being under the beautiful, blinding, assuaging cloak of drink—should such a hypothetical opportunity still arise.

With Dylan it was roughly the same pattern of behaviour, except that it was my own, my very own, nobody else's Dylan participating in it. Yes, I was exclusively possessive about him. Just as we never spent a single evening (that I can remember) alone together at home, so we never went to bed sober. He was just as shy as I was, though he kept it better hidden than I could, and he had great difficulty whipping his trousers off at the double, flinging them in a zig-zagging pyramid on the floor and sliding, in his long flannel to-his-knees shirt, under the sheets. A shivering slippery tiny top-heavy tadpole clinging to and digging into my buxom rotundity for dear divine life.

When I reminisce on our Arabian nights together, to rock the world with wonderment at my sleeping with a god, I am confronted with the conflicting images of ritualistic fights to the death on the floor of our bedroom at night, on a seasick sea, followed by the ecstatically tenderest of reconciliations. I am confronted by four fists—Dylan's two delicate tapering ones and my two square ones—clenched in each other's bushes of kissing curls, tearing them out by the roots, and banging each other's heads as hard as we could, with drink-enraged force, on the old splintering boards of our bedroom. We were just about equal in length and strength, though Dylan insisted he was longer than me and I insisted I was stronger than him. Don't tell me it was nothing but a bit of innocent love-play. No doubt the green daggers of jealousy and of suspected infidelities had been at work, since that one unacceptable breach of faith was the only true bone of contention between us. But unfortunately we both felt that what we did apart, unseen by the other, was quite another matter, not to be taken seriously at all. For each of us it was a mere passing incident, on a different, infinitely lower scale than our concrete-solid immortal love. But for the other one—and this held for both of us—it was a deadly sin punishable by bloody death. These regular nightly frenzied duels, whatever they were about, served at least to hack down the jagged discord between us, to break through the thickets and nettles of drink and clear the air and our heads for the foreseeable grand finale: our everlasting supernatural love together. We cradled in each other's arms with unbelievable tenderness, in our worn-out exhaustion afterwards, till we dropped off, two lovable, curly heads side by side on white pillows, into a perfectly peaceful, innocent unblemished sleep.

Anybody who happened to look in on us could have been excused for concluding that there lay the ideal loving couple in their perfect married bliss, with no puff of cloud on their serene horizon. Just how misleading can circumstantial evidence be! We were lying, it is true, in the sense of lying down; but we were also lying, it is equally true, in the sense of telling a lie. Behind our eyelids, the next day's betrayals were already taking shape. Not till the clattering morning came, bulldozing open our booze-bleary eyes and depositing its load of money worries on our doorstep, did we reluctantly return to evil consciousness.

We were basically good, innocent and loving each other till kingdom came. But by the time drink had got itself nastily circulating in our systems, by our plodding away at it all through the dull day (such industrious tenacity would have been praiseworthy in any other working capacity), we were transformed from angels into fiends. Perhaps I should add that my propensity for fiendishness was more fiendish than Dylan's, whose natural-born nature was nicer and more peaceable than mine. He tended to become soft and sentimental when drunk; but drink makes fiends or fools of us all, and there is not a lot to choose between the two.

The extraordinary factor in our drinking, which was done with the punctilious sense of duty of an aspiring clerk clocking into the office dead on time, is that never once did it occur to either of us to blame drink for any of our difficulties, starting with our perennial money troubles. So we lived in wilful destitution, because whatever we received, even if it had been a million pounds (our brains boggled beyond a million), it all went in the same monotonous way: down the drain of drink. Which sapped us, not only of all our money, but of all our wits, brains, blood, hearts, souls and all too soon of Dylan's life.

Not only did I make no attempt at controlling his drinking, I valiantly attempted to out-drink him. My preposterous valour, if nothing else, should be admired. I was cursed with a cast-iron stomach, which meant that all the alcohol that went into it stayed in, then painstakingly circulated through all my body, spreading its damage steadily and unremittingly, with no recuperative pause in which to rebuild my defences. And I kept my end up. For every pint of draught bitter and mild (black and tan) that Dylan knocked back, I responded with a double Scotch and ginger ale, and Dylan, when he was on the cure in the country, drank roughly twenty pints a night.

Drinking on tick was one (I am tempted to say the chief one, in Dylan's case) of the advantages of living in a small town. The neighbours would do anything (even pay if driven hard enough) and forgive anything just for a spark of entertainment. And with Dylan the sparks always flew. Our neighbours loved and accepted him in the simplest kind of way: as a brother. Not so much as their own blood brother, whom they might loathe the sight of, but as a brother after their own hearts.

I, too, got on all right with the local people; a bit too all right, one might have said. There was an instinctive kinship between us. At the daily drinking sessions round the table in the bow window of our pub, I piped down at Dylan's unspoken order. I had no choice really, and could not have got a word in edgeways had I tried. It bred in me an abscess of contempt that has not been lanced to this day. And I looked —to my disgust, for I longed to look the opposite—the epitome of a pink-cheeked, corn-haired, bursting-at-the-seams milkmaid, a deadly combination of silence and succulence that could hardly fail to make me palatable to the locals.

In theory, as a good conventional little wife (though it must be clear by now that I fitted that role about as well as a bull fits into a china shop), I should have been nagging Dylan about his ruinous drinking: ruinous to his finances, ruinous to his work and ruinous to his health. I should have been swearing my head off at him night and day to desist, to moderate like his father, to go easy, to stop dragging himself and his family into degradation and ruin. I should have been patiently sitting at home darning his socks, waiting for him with his supper on the hob, with his warmed slippers laid out neatly by his cushy armchair, on a plush-sinking red-flowered carpet beside a glowing red-coaled fireplace, his pipe and matches at the ready. How he would have lapped it all up, as his natural, all-in-the-day's-work due. Oh yes, Dylan was a rigid traditionalist, especially where males' rights and females' lack of rights were concerned.

My sole comfort for not being all that I should have been is that had I been all those good conventional things, I would never have seen Dylan again. I would be patiently waiting for him still with his supper on the hob, slightly frizzled-up by now, to be sure. The waiting meal and my waiting self would have been the two symbols of the rewards of virtue!

There are no quick exits, no easy ways out, from the drinking life. Except the one Dylan took. Only the non-alcoholic can really enjoy his drink. The alcoholic nearly burns himself up for the need of more fire inside him. This lengthy process is what I consider happened to me, is what made me—if not a born alcoholic, the next best thing to it—one who by sheer hard work achieves the same goal, achieves it even more securely by dint of praiseworthy perseverance.

It was my physical strength that was the trouble. Thanks to all that disgusting goat's milk that our mother pumped down her three barbarian daughters' throats, I was embarrassingly strong; and when my natural strength was reinforced by the artificial strength of alcohol, I became a formidable opponent.

At a certain more advanced, less artistic stage in the drinking proceedings, I would hurl myself across the room at some inoffensive man, with the force and cutting edge of a recklessly hurled boomerang. Whether it was with the intention of beating him to a pulp and slapping him dead, which I was perfectly capable of doing, or of making an amorous pass, it was hard to say. I was never quite sure myself. Nor was he. He was more frightened than flattered and usually took off at a run. He could not understand, the uneducated dolt, that violence was only the first round of my subtle approach. Very few of my scapegoats stuck it out till the second round— either out of curiosity or courage. My beast was now in full possession of me and had completely outed my sober shrinking-violet self—and my beast had no prudishness. The ill-confined desire of my snarling beast was to lash out and get into a fight. I cannot explain what were the medical motives behind my beast's overriding desire—but to alcoholics there is nothing new in this fearful transformation. The personality switches from white to black through alcohol's penetration of the organic machinery of the individual.

The extent of my shrinking-violet self's subjection to drink can be accurately gauged by my having no recollection whatsoever of that momentous girlhood experience—the robbing of my virginity. It could have been anybody, at any time; I had not felt a thing. But by whom, if only as a point of interest, by whom? I worried sometimes at these unfillable blanks in my memory and that they occurred so soon. The beginning of blackouts so soon was a most ominous alcoholic sign.

The truth, as they say, will come out all right in drink. But it is the truth of the devil, the beast in all of us. God's truth, the good truth, hides its face when the devil's truth in drink takes over, which explains the frightful remorse and guilt in the morning. It is God's truth, the good truth, coming back to reprove its recalcitrant child. Not so gently either: unmercifully! Not to mention the physical reverberations and disturbances that go along with (and are so admirably in tune with) the moral discomfiture. It is not my fault if all the conventional platitudes are dead true. Drinking turned out to be my devil. And to be potent the devil must have a potent power. And what more potent potion can he wield than alcohol?

2

A Cocktail of Words and Drink

Between the wordy warmth of his spontaneous mother and the contained restraint of his gentleman father, Dylan could hardly have failed to be moulded into that incalculable being: a poet. I suppose, reluctantly, that I looked to him like a younger version of his mother: she was a simple, good-natured farmer's daughter who never stopped talking, who gabbled all the time in a Welsh up-and-down lilt. *Looked* like her, I said, not *was* like her. For I hardly talked at all and was infinitely pretentious deep inside, while she was not at all. But Dylan had no interest in what was going on inside me; the flesh-and-blood object was good enough for him.

They say that spoilt, coddled and cossetted sons marry their mothers all over again. Well, Dylan made a mistake when he picked me if that was what he wanted. Devil a lot of spoiling, coddling and cossetting he got out of me! I was not going to let him see that down in the caverns of my being he sometimes stirred in me a murmuring source of gently bubbling love for him. I was much too riddled with stupid Irish

false pride, which came from an atavistic fear of being hurt
and which went with the same stupid Irish fear of the plea-
sures of the flesh. We both, as painful and presumptuous
Celts, suffered from a strong puritanical streak which we
stifled with overdoses of alcohol. Dylan, who had read everything, knew nearly all the erotic stuff in print, and fancied
himself no end as an erotic dog. But his doggish erotism was
displayed chiefly on paper or in the spoken word. Its fascination for him was always more in words than in physical performance. For one thing, by the time he got around to
putting his words into his performance, there was not much
left erect with which to perform.

I had spent a year in Paris, starving in a garret with a
Russian painter. I considered this to be sophisticated, but very
few of the sceptics that always surrounded us believed me, for
it was just the sort of lie they were most prone to invent themselves. In truth, neither of us had got much further than the
birds-and-bees.

Dylan had only to see a word standing all on its own than
he had to break his brain obscuring it with a downpour of
more superimposed words. He would never say anything in a
straightforward manner. Instead, he would mix words up, put
them the wrong way around, back to front, upside down, thus
tying them in impossible knots. Why, for instance, couldn't
he simply answer what cinema he had been to, instead of
(without any benefit to himself in the lie) making up another
cinema and a different film? He wrapped the tameness of
reality in the convolutions of his mind. It was obviously
easier for him to say in a complicated way what he did not
mean than to say in a simple way what he did mean. It could
be thought of as unnecessary invention or charming fantasy. I
simply called him a chronic liar.

He was both simple and complex. It took him a long and
laborious time to work through his wordy complications, to
clean his decks of an unserviceable clutter of words (when he

loved each one separately so much and could not bear to part with his special favourites), and to move towards his eventual singing simplicity.

The simplicity of every truly great artist seems so spontaneous that lesser artists say to themselves, "There is nothing to it"—until they have tried it. In fact, it requires a systematic selection of chosen words and a merciless elimination of scrapped ones. In his development as a true artist, Dylan was greatly aided by his schoolteacher father's scholarly and scrupulous erudition which, even though Dylan feigned to spurn it, gave him the essential discipline of his craft.

There is, of course, a danger to great simplicity: that it will not, of necessity, be great. It might be simply simple and that is all. There are two types of simplicity: the unconscious kind of the genuinely simple person (if such a person still exists), which can be good or bad—more likely bad; and the conscious kind of the person with a complex mechanism who has worked hard to attain his simplicity. Like the convert's faith, this second type is more valuable artistically. Instead of being a taken-for-granted gift, it is a passionately worked-for conviction.

Dylan possessed both the taken-for-granted gift and the passionately worked-for conviction. Even if he worked only spasmodically and erratically (when he was exiled, half dead, back to my nearly permanent penitential banishment), his conviction still bravely persisted. Even when it appeared that he was doing his damnedest to kill his gift, it was quietly working away inside his head.

It was his only real reason for living. But it was also his only real reason for dying: the death of his gift. Every honest-to-God artist knows the excruciating price that must be paid if he can do no less than create. This is why he avoids creating. Dylan had that terrible necessity to escape, if only temporarily, from the slavery of his gift.

Unconsciously, both of us strived to keep it at bay, to

annul it. Only when we were completely wrecked by alcohol did we retire to the country to fall back on the sullen art and craft of patiently, painfully fitting and knitting words together into poetry.

We both knew the mysterious gift was there, rooted in Dylan's soul, but we had an unwritten understanding never to mention it. It came partly from Dylan's deference to my ignorance of poetry, and partly from Dylan's transparent pretence to be a man of the people. He did not like talking intellectually—though he could do so very competently if he wanted to. He was afraid, I think, that the words would shrink, shrivel up, lose their original sheen, with too much analysis.

I avoided Dylan's writing work like a dangerous plague. I was afraid it might contaminate my precious personal integrity if I let it get too close to me. In my opinion the worst accusation that could be made by one artist against another was that the other—that is myself—was influenced by, was under the self-diminishing spell of, Dylan's position and work. Not that I had any pretentions then of being a writer myself. God forbid! I was still on my dancing kick. As I said, we were both always absolutely sure that Dylan was going to be the supreme poet of all time and I was going to be the supreme dancer of all time. Although to ears other than mine this bold statement may have rung a little less true, I was always absolutely sure of it. There was no limit to my vain personal aspirations—none at all. It never occurred to me that the drinking life was not a suitable training-ground for the premier dancer of the age. Nor was a drunken dancer inspired by the Dutch courage of alcohol at her scintillating best.

Notwithstanding our blatant poverty, I was always pestering Dylan about getting me a large studio in which to practise my dancing. Dylan, as impractical as myself, would kindly and seriously try to find one, or intend to do so. We never got one! Such unquestioning faith in my art, in the midst of our poverty, our children and our curse of drinking, I find in retrospect not only too hard to believe but pitiably touching.

Some time later, a misguided idiot said I had a "feeling for words." And in those past unthinking days a feeling for words or a feeling for colour was quite enough to lead a romantic young lady with no education to set herself up as a new Dostoevsky or a future van Gogh. When I would finally produce, in acute embarrassment, four tortured lines for his inspection, Dylan would calmly reply: "Yes, very good; why don't you work on them?" If only he had known how long I had already struggled with them, counting the syllables! I thought they were a finished poem.

A very few times, because I was so maddeningly baffled, I asked him outright: "What is a poem anyhow? How is it made? What makes a poem a poem?" He said there were no set-down rules for modern poetry. I never got a more satisfactory answer out of him than "Either you can feel it or you can't." That was a hell of a lot of use to my logical way of working things out. So one collection of random words put hearingly in the right place was a poem. But the same collection of random words put deafly in the wrong place was not a poem. That was a hopelessly abstract definition for me! Not even rhyme, he said, was necessary; though he did it himself in all sorts of unexpected odd places. And the length of the lines? Purely arbitrary. So we were back to my famous old "feeling" again. But I knew that the "feeling" alone was not enough. It had to be put together, set into motion. Maybe, I thought afterwards, he was deliberately keeping essential information from me, jealously guarding his secret (I couldn't blame him if he was) for fear of a would-be, pseudo-intellectual wife driving him crazy; a fear of his dumb bouncing milkmaid turning into a bespectacled bluestocking. His terror of intellectual women was on the same primitive level as his terror of mice. He should have known me better: there was not an inkspot of a hint then of such an improbable transformation. Not for another twenty years or so anyhow! And then he would not be there—blessedly for him—to witness his shame for me.

In the world of artists, the most unrewarding job is to be the wife of a famous artist, because whatever she does to develop her own separate personality appears inevitably as a pale imitation of what he has done. And whether she is envious or not of his fame (and let's face it, it is very difficult for her not to be), she is automatically dubbed an envious cat. I disliked intensely my secondary role. I strongly wanted Dylan to have his glory, but I did not like to bask in its secondary rays. Reflected glory for me has always been an intolerable ignominy. All I wished was to be my very own little sun, and not such a little sun at that; rather, let me say modestly, a blazing meteor.

It was all very well my deciding I was going to be better than Isadora Duncan, whose undisciplined slovenliness I severely disapproved of (oh yes, I was as keen a disciplinarian in my art as Dylan was a traditionalist in his), but circumstances were not in my favour. Drunken dancing to a drunken audience at pub-closing time was not the peak of polished grace and virtuosity. If there seemed to be a marked discrepancy between our orderly beliefs and our disorderly behaviour, we could not help it: that was the way it was. Had we been sober people, we would have been visibly quite different.

There always came a fatal moment in the evening's drinking when I could no longer hold back my colossal straining-at-the-leash vitality. Of its own accord, without my volition, it suddenly broke loose, leapt into the air and furiously struck out. My painfully strapped-in limbs, kept too long in a standing or sitting posture, struck out blindly, wildly, jubilantly. At last I had killed, with the unfailing lethal drink, the last vestiges of my self-consciousness. And I didn't give a damn what anybody thought. I was perfectly sure that after my dazzling performance the world would never again be the same dull place. It would be changed unrecognizably into a theatre of clamorous applause. There was no hated sex, no trace of invitation in my dancing. It was purely selfish—for the perfection of myself alone and the liberation of my spirit. Though I hesitate to use such a deadly uncompromising little three-letter word, it was, I believe, a surging "joy." It was all the vital sap in my being, plus the extra vital sap in the bottle, of course, springing into inexpressible life.

I believe I knew true joy when, by some happy chance, I was only with the music and the music was only with me. It was the old enigma: which came first, the music or me? We were welded together indissolubly. I could feel the music running through me as if I was a tunnel, and nothing could stop me leaping to my feet and letting fly. It was the music moving in me, not me moving to the music. It was an ecstatic joy that I knew only in absolute privacy or deflowered by drink, clumsily falling all over the place in public.

When I viewed my public in sobriety, I froze up in fright and couldn't budge an inch. I was paralysed with shyness. That wretched shyness was responsible for some of my and Dylan's worst outrages: the fruit of our attempts at assassinating it. It was the waste, the ghastly waste, that I resented most about our drinking, or rather that I *now* resent most. But *waste* is the word that best sums up that incalculable devastation and havoc of our lives.

Once hooked by the drinking spiderweb, all anti-drinking arguments are irrelevant. Drink is an impure and murderous thing that can't be done without. Useless to prate or pray or preach against the evil of drink, for the evil itself has taken over; it is in possession of the drinker's soul.

From the start, Dylan had all the proverbial propensities attributed to a born alcoholic. He was weak by nature, lazy by habit and decadent by inclination. But he certainly did not suffer from a lack of love at home, deprivation of any kind or rejection by anybody: the usual excuses of the born alcoholic.

He suffered from the well-meaning, chit-chattering reverse: from being spoilt to death by his mother as her youngest, only, small and delicate, sweetest cherub son. Finally, in furious desperation at her incessant admonitions about his well-being, he would pick up the nearest large book, a dictionary or an encyclopedia, and hurl it at his mother's head. She was never bothered by the books: she was quite used to their flying around. As long as she didn't have to look inside them.

Then Dylan would rush across the road to his substitute mother: the landlady of the main pub in town, whom I swear he loved with a far deeper and more reverent devotion than his real mother. Not because she was any better looking (she was an uglier version of his own) but simply because she was *not* his own. She was the Sacred Cow, the credit-giving landlady of his pub-home, to whom he recounted what a misunderstood genius had to endure in the nattering swamps of domestic pettiness. The crafty landlady, devoted to him too, in return regaled him with the previous night's spicy scandals, which he sucked up for future reference like a hungry vacuum cleaner.

Who would have thought that our sleepy little town woke up at nightfall, after the "mythical" closing-time (there was no closing-time in our thirteen pubs), to such blood-curdling goings-on? Husband-beating, by those swarthy brawny-armed cockle women of their sloshed slinking-in-late husbands, was a perfectly normal regular occurrence in their City of Laughter, as they liked to call Laugharne. There were neurotics by the dozen and incest was all the rage.

In addition to the coddling he received from his mother and the landlady, Dylan expected me to act as muse and audience. Notwithstanding his low opinion of women's minds and the fact that I was acutely reluctant to play the part he forced on me, I acted as a convenient guinea pig for him in our bogs—where, admittedly, there was no literary competition even for guinea pigs. Dylan would stride into the kitchen bristling with enthusiasm and flapping his latest poem straight from the mint. He would relentlessly pin me down at the sink where I was scrubbing, in my perfectionist manner, a pile of snowily frothing nappies. Impervious to both my wriggling embarrassment and the squalor on the floor surrounding us, he would start booming and intoning in his deep bass voice what to me sounded like a never-ending sermon of senseless, jumbled, mumbled, confusing, strung-together words. I instinctively switched off my mind. It did not go in one ear and out the other; it never even got in my first ear, an ear which was firmly blocked against any invasion of its fighting integrity, which was terrified of being drowned in Dylan's ocean of words.

When at long last the drone of buzzing words stopped and I was practically seething with impatience, he would pop the million-dollar question: what did *I* think of it? I was flabbergasted; I did not know what to reply. I did not want to hurt his feelings. I knew, though, that I did not understand his poem and that it was my loss, not his. So I would answer at random, playing for time, pleading my flagrant ignorance of all writing of any enduring consequence, falling into cowardly compromise. Finally, with inordinate feebleness, I came out with: "I like the sound of it, but I could not get the sense." And perhaps I would tentatively add, did it not seem to him that there were a few too many words piled on top of the crushing others? The understatement of the age. But he was utterly indifferent really. He was not even listening to my muttered reaction. He was far too engrossed in his still-sizzling and bubbling creation to take any real notice of silly little comments I might hesitantly put in. He simply wanted to get his great gobstopper off his heaving chest, to spit it out of his system for his own personal satisfaction.

He would then do me the honour of asking which words I liked best or what I would put in their place, or add to them. As though it was humanly possible to add anything more to that already overladen, toppling-over mountain of richly dripping words. It could benefit only from a cold-blooded subtraction of beautiful but superfluous words. But funnily enough, when I did make some half-hearted suggestion out of the blue, just to please him, he quite often inserted it and left it there—although it would hardly be noticeable among that motley crowd of his, except to us.

There is still a lot to be said in favour of asking an ignoramus for advice: it serves to show the vacillating creator that what he put down originally was right. Had he asked a knowledgeable person for advice, he could not have remained so sure he was right.

Even though I kept my ear firmly blocked against any dangerous infiltration of Dylan's powerful and disturbing music of poetry, certain of his best-known lines did somehow get past my barricades to haunt me in my solitude. " 'And Death shall have no dominion…' *indeed*!" I would say to myself. He could make the biggest lie on earth sound true.

While most reputable writers affect to spurn the critics' reviews, it is very difficult, if not impossible, even for them not to be influenced by what the critics say. Dylan was no exception in this respect. He never would have admitted that he cared one tuppenny hoot about what they said: he ostensibly despised the whole envious breed. Yet he was intrigued and flattered by some of the extraordinary interpretations of his contradictory lines by these connoisseurs. Sometimes, after reading them, he would say: "Yes, that is a most ingenious idea. Maybe I did really mean that. Wish I had thought of it!" He was fascinated also by their imputations of the influence on his work of certain ancient classics which sometimes Dylan had not even read. But rather than admit his ignorance, he would immediately remedy the deficiency, get hold of the boring book and plough or skip through it.

He was a great one at skipping through books, and when early on he was reviewing books for a few extra pounds, he

would go through four or five a day with ease, in his extremely limited spare time from drinking. A book that would take
me at least three months of regular nightly plodding through,
he would polish off at a sitting. And the most irritating thing
about it was that I, who after all my hard work should have
known the book much more thoroughly and profoundly than
he did, knew much less. He was much more familiar with it,
down to the smallest details.

Dylan would read to me in bed at night too, on more
sober or semi-sober (which is to say flat broke) occasions. He
did so in the most conventional manner in the world, as
though we were the most conventional couple in the world.
And so we were, in fact, though Dylan was very careful to
keep our dark secret well hidden. He read the interminable
works of Dickens, for whom he had an exaggerated passion;
Thackeray, I can't think why; Blake, whom he worshipped;
and the poems of Lawrence, Hardy, Donne and many more I
can only half remember. Although I found it a lot easier to listen to these more or less straightforward writers than to
Dylan's stuff (anything was easier than his stuff), I was always
the world's worst listener. To listen properly one must be able
to forget oneself, and that was the hardest thing for me to do.
I could never do that.

However, I did deeply appreciate (not that I would have
dreamt of telling him so) how beautifully he read. He took as
many pains for me alone as he would have done at a public
reading. He read even more quietly and beautifully than usual
because he was more relaxed. However, it was a bit like the
old proverb as far as I was concerned: God gives the biscuit to
those without teeth to chew on it.

Whatever our secret conventional tendencies, we hid them
in public beneath our extraordinary style and our defiant way
of presenting ourselves. We managed to combine our natural
predilections for bright striking colours, mixed contrarily to
catch the eye, with the mundane limitations of necessity. We

had no money to buy the smart, sober, matching clothes that we secretly longed for but could never have. So, in protest against our penury, to draw attention to our paupery, to flaunt it in the face of respectable people, to shame them by it and to make them buy drinks for us, we draped ourselves in colourful contrasting rags.

I sometimes think we were the original hippies and that all the later ones were imitations. It wasn't that we believed in a saintly hippy mission (though there is no denying we enjoyed our parts as downtrodden outcasts from society). The only other choice was to be slaving ants. Of the two, the latter definitely appealed to us least. Besides, how could someone like Dylan, a uniquely creative artist and literally nothing else, be expected to waste his huge talent slaving at some stupid deadening job? The only job I could have got was high-kicking in the front line of the chorus at the London Palladium. I was always the best dancer but could not sing, which was a big handicap for the plum shows. But that was before I met Dylan. After that, I became paralysed and forgot which leg went up next. Standing there baffled in the middle, I was the only stationary girl in a long line of high-kickers. Shortly afterwards I got the sack with no reasons given; I am only just beginning to guess what those reasons could possibly have been.

The patches on our clothing were not sewn on for picturesque decoration. Nor were the dirt and the smell applied for extra genuine flavour. They grew there, gradually, in the soil of our bohemian way of life. We would stop dead in the middle of a busy, traffic-hooting street and start tearing and ripping at ourselves, in the most indelicate places, like two dressed-up chimps from the zoo. We couldn't help it, the itching was too strong for us. Later we always carried with us a large tin of sulphur ointment (the only cure known to us for the common itch) with which we generously sullied the sheets of whatever host had been so foolishly gracious as to have us as their ungracious house-guests.

The bohemian life perhaps appeared glamorous to a very far-off onlooker, but not for all the tea in China, or more to the point, for all the wine in the Rhine, seductively tempting as it sounds, would I go back to it. It is the dim memory of it, most of all, that keeps me moving on the dry barren path of abstemiousness.

Nor was there with us a concealed pocket of family funds to fall back on when the bluff of assumed poverty wore too dreadfully thin. We were as poor as the rags we stood up in and as rich as the drink made us. So long as it kept us standing up. Well, we did receive one pound a week from my mother, not a big sum even in those distant days. Plus an occasional fiver from Dylan's father, when he could scrape it together out of his meagre schoolmaster's pension. And the highbrow poems that had taken Dylan several months to work on, and that no ordinary body could understand and only highbrows guessed at, were published in small money-less literary magazines, and fetched no more than a couple of pathetic quid at that time. They were not exactly doing a roaring trade. The payment for one poem was ludicrously out of all proportion to the enormous effort and time that Dylan put into it.

The truth of the matter was that a penniless poet should never get married, let alone allow himself, even accidentally, to make a family. And no woman should be such a fool as to marry a penniless poet! No other woman would have. That was the fatal error and, incidentally, the lucky miracle from the start. But if truth be told, we were quick to spend whatever sums of money were given to us by our long-suffering patronesses. There was never enough for our insatiable thirsts, for our incorrigible drinking habits. As soon as we got a little extra lump, we not only treated ourselves handsomely to the best in the house, but loved to call out, "Drinks on us all round!" We loved to share our new-found, though short-lived, prosperity. It gave us the illusion of being good inside. The thought that the money that we were so generously spending on our old cronies and lifelong buddies and best pals was not really our money, but money that belonged to our special patroness who was trying to help us, never seemed to ring any guilty tinkle of bells in our cloud-stuffed heads. Cloud-stuffed is a polite way of describing the drink-soaked blotting paper that was lodged in our heads and through which no tinkling of conscience was permitted to penetrate.

Our constant penury led me to other inventive ways. My method of making a shirt for Dylan was to get a square of checked cotton (a tablecloth would do fine), fold it over longways then shortways, cut a slit for the head on the folded side, cut an angular wedge out for the sleeves on the outside edge (I had never heard of sewing in sleeves), then open it out and sew up the two side seams first on the right side then on the wrong side, for double strength, with my meticulous French sewing, about the only thing I had ever learned from our string of useless French governesses. And, presto, that was it. Then the poor dab Dylan proudly wore this absurd garment and told everybody his clever wife had just run it up by plying her industrious needle. It was I, not he, who was slightly shamefaced at the clownish figure I had made Dylan cut and by my own hopeless inefficiency.

No house was safe from my speculative eyes, which roamed up and down the flowery curtains, seeing them sinuously wrapped around me in becoming folds, or which pensively gazed at a Persian rug or polar bear skin laid out on the floor for my approval. Would they not make a super dramatic cloak for Dylan to make his next entry into the hushed-in-awe rabble of the pub?

The blankets and eiderdowns and coverings of the beds were the most obvious winter coats for us. Many of the richer, more exotic ones mysteriously disappeared—to the innocent perplexity of their owners. We were such practised experts at cashing in on our misleading baby faces and curly locks all aglow with dewy innocence that nobody would have had the nerve to accuse such sweet sucklings of theft! And of course we joined in the worried speculations about how the rowdy soldiers from the camp nearby could have broken in and pinched the loot... We were full of ingenious suggestions. Keen as I was on the strict undeviating truth, there were certain cases when the survival of the weakest (who were usually the fittest to reason) was at stake and a wee little white lie could not be avoided.

Dylan's touching belief in my domestic abilities (which were less than nil) extended to my cooking prowess. And this took an even greater faith than believing in the invisible. It was also much nearer to his heart, since the heart, one is told, is approached through the belly. It had been so dinned into him that Mother's cooking was best that regardless of which "Mother" was presiding at the table he unquestioningly believed it. For anybody but him this mother's cooking was unquestionably the worst. And, strangely enough, though few people saw him do it, he liked eating. He enjoyed his special kinds of food, typical Welsh things like faggots and peas, tripe and onions (though it was always leeks in Wales); he adored laver bread, the bread of the sea, and most of all, especially in our cockle town, cockles. Sunken cockles, scraped by rough hands from their mud homes, were thrown in the heat of a dry frying pan, rattled to make them spit out the mud and finally spread on home-baked bread with yellow salted butter. More delicious than all the Russian caviar...

I can still see Dylan's mother now in her eternal gesture of cutting endless slices of that delicious bread and butter: so thin, as she told Dylan as a child and as she told our children later, that you could see London through it. Those habit-making traditions, the same old ritual year after year, made a cradling background for Dylan that I had not. And though they may be dull and monotonous for a bright young spark to live in, they are invaluable roots to suck the sap from, excellent night fodder from which to weave dreams; the best rock-bottom foundation for a rebellious spirit—if for nothing else than to rebel against.

For no self-respecting artist could call himself an artist unless he had fiercely rebelled against something. And Dylan, with all his powers of invention, was very hard put to invent sufficient provocations, suppressions, frustrations, clanking chains holding him down and restricting his inspiration to justify his essential rebellion: there were none. His provincial background, which he very much belonged to and liked (at least the comforts of it), and which he fitted into as snugly as a bug in a rug, was not at all a convincing enough excuse for his out-of-all-proportion explosion of sound and fury.

I, on the contrary, came from my emancipated background, and rebelled against my lack of chains, lack of education, lack of religion, lack of discipline or any guiding principles whatsoever. Not even the domestic arts or the social graces were taught to me and my sisters. Our optimistic mother simply told us that we would all marry rich men and be waited upon by servants. She was a trifle out of date, and, it need hardly be said, not one of us did marry a rich man and not one of us was capable of boiling an egg. We all had to start from scratch building our houses on foundations of sand. And so I had no alternative: marry either a rich man or an ordinary common Englishman.

I will now change the subject from Dylan: never-to-be-forgotten, eternal great poet. Drunk, sober, lying, thieving, unfaithful to me, but all the more human for his disgraceful faults. I will talk of how I spent my carefree childhood with my sisters Nicolette and Brigit and, on special occasions, with my glamorous brother, John, home from the Royal Navy.

childhood

3
The Macnamaras

My father, Francis Macnamara (known as Fireball Macnamara), came from the fairyland of the west of Ireland in County Clare. My mother was half Irish and half French. My father was known in all the surrounding country and in Dublin as well as one of the giant-sized classic charmers: an eloquently declaiming blarney-man. It was from him that I developed my dislike and mistrust of all professional charmers by whom it was my inescapable destiny to be pursued all my life.

I was born in Hammersmith, London. Later on we moved to Ringwood, a small market town near the New Forest in Hampshire. After years of pleading with our super-refined mother to be sent to a proper school like other children, my sisters and I were sent to the nearby Parents' National Education Union. Although more like a kindergarten than a serious school, it was a great improvement on the series of French governesses our mother insisted on having imported from France to give us a touch of class. I think Mother had finally realized that, besides being utterly useless as far as our education was concerned, the governesses were capable only of playing with the cats and going to bed with my beautiful brother, John, who did his utmost to satisfy their sex-starved condition. She thus gave up her pretensions of French culture, and coldly banished them.

But the third governess was a wily devil. At the moment of departure, she was nowhere to be found, and the taxi had to leave without her. When Brigit and I came in at tea-time, after a bracing walk over the heather-purpled moors to liberate ourselves from the distinctive smell of our governesses, there she was again, the third governess, small as life, crouched over the glowing red stove, playing with her cats again and happily reading Proust. She was quite immovable. She hung around until John, who just doted on tiny women with clusters of chicken bones, asked her to marry him! Her name was Enriette and she was only too delighted, of course. It was just what she had schemed and waited for. After John's proposal of marriage, she could not move out from the house fast enough.

In that little day school, our first school of any kind, we were supremely happy, chiefly because, for the first time in our lives, we were given a regular pattern to follow and set occupations at fixed times. We lapped it up. It was so much easier, lazier, to live in that regular way. One did not have to think what to do or how to do it; one simply did, in the best way one could, what was laid down to do.

Having other children around gave us unbounded joy. We could not believe our eyes. We were no longer alone, penned off in our goat-fold! And it gave us a most satisfactory feeling to have a purpose in life and to belong to something bigger than ourselves, even if that purpose was not a very profound one. It lifted a great weight of responsibility off our shoulders. At home, we had to search daily for our occupations and invent them ourselves in a timelessly expanding day. I constantly wailed to our mother, "I don't know what to do." To which our mother would most likely reply: "Go and weed the garden path," or something equally inspiring, and my heart would sink down into my boots.

After not knowing what to do next, it was a great relief to be pinned down to something definite. We sat around in small groups on benches at a long wooden table with all the paraphernalia of our handiwork laid out in front of us. We were fascinated, but bewildered too, by the unfamiliar objects. First of all, we made comparatively easy raffia mats. Luckily, the pattern was already indicated on the matting, but our hands, unaccustomed to such meticulous work, were all bungling thumbs at the start. With practice, however, and deep concentration, even us country yokels managed to get the hang of it at last, to our enormous satisfaction.

Then there was the much more difficult task of making beaded bags. We had, first of all, to thread the many coloured beads on strong cotton thread; that part was easy and fun. But then we had to sew the strings of beads, firmly, to dainty evening bags. For whom and for what purpose it was impossible to tell—certainly not for our modest Quaker teachers. And here is where the trouble started, and where our total lack of domestic skills was glaringly exposed. Our fingers, stiff as ramrods from tugging at the hard mouths of horses, refused to ply our needles. They had hardly ever held a needle previously, except for piercing holes in birds' eggs. So it was that we finally presented, with some trepidation, a most awkward and clumsy job of work. Our patient sister teachers never reproved us but simply encouraged us to keep on trying.

Teachers like them are gold; they make their pupils enjoy learning. They are as rare as happy marriages. They possess both the knowledge and the know-how to impart that knowledge to those thirsty souls who have an overriding desire to learn.

But of all our handiwork, we loved best making *woolly*

balls! For a start, we were each handed a circular piece of cardboard with a large round hole in the middle. We had to go over and under the hole with our bodkin of wools and, simultaneously, round and round the edges of the cardboard, until the hole was crammed full of varicoloured wools. Then came the big moment when we cut open all the wool round the circumference of the cardboard. The wool, thus liberated, shot itself loose and expanded into a quivering ball before our wondering eyes. We could hardly bear to part with these fluffy balls and, secretly, longed to keep them for ourselves. They were like rainbows rolled up into a ball.

There were also nature walks once or twice a week, to get us in the open air and keep us informed about plants and trees. We had little notebooks and pencils to write down the names of the wild flowers growing under the hedges on the sides of the lane. We knew hardly any of their proper names and had to ask the teacher for information on nearly every flower we picked. So much for our mystical involvement with nature! We did not even know the correct names of the simple hedgerow flowers.

When we got back to the school, we were made to dissect our collections or specimens and give names to their various parts. The teacher then explained the functions of those parts, which, need I repeat, was hot news for us. Then we were made to draw in our drawing books, then paint in them, in watercolours, very carefully, all the intricate details of our specimen under observation. This very exacting work was good for us and gave us a great sense of achievement when we saw the finished annotated specimen straggling all over the page. Although we had lived in the midst of nature nearly all our lives, we had never named it, dissected it or put it on paper, and it was fun. It was a revelation to us!

I cannot recall ever being taught any actual lessons or normal school subjects by Miss Lydia or Miss Susan. Which may account for our happiness in being there. What we did learn

was so much more interesting and useful to us. We loved
making those elementary but instructive little fabrications; we
were happy in our little day school and, miracle upon miracle,
we had friends at last of our own age whom we could invite
back to our house to play games with us. Despite our excitement at the prospect of playing with children from our
school, we all had hidden misgivings about bringing them
back into our rustic, rough, uncouth and disorderly home.
We knew that we were in some way different from these foreign children—different for the worse, it goes without saying.
We hated this difference between us and them and the sense
of isolation that it gave us. We had no common language, no
small talk, with these conventional children. We were
stumped, inarticulate. We wanted only to be exactly like them
in every minute detail, especially in their manner of dress,
which we found so devastatingly attractive and such a telling
contrast to ours. We wanted to be, in mode and manner,
indistinguishable from them. What a hope we had! Never in
a million years, with the best will in the world, could we have
fitted into the neat narrow niches of preordained conformity.
We were not made of the same malleable stuff. With our wild
upbringing, we could never have stood the constriction and,
in no time at all, we would have blown our tops and escaped.
Or wilted and shrivelled up like pressed wild flowers between
the pages of a book.

It never occurred to us then that though we were not like
these enviable children (nor ever would be), we might have
something good in our own right, something that they had
not got. No such far-fetched idea ever entered our numb-
skulls. We had set our craving hearts on living like them on
the smooth polished surface of life, and never on pain of
death dropping one inch below the ice-rink surface. We
wanted little black books packed with our engagements for
weeks ahead.

This premeditated planning of one's life, this laying out

in advance of all the future engagements in one's life, was a completely new and very exciting thought for us, who never knew from one day to the next what was in store. It struck us as the perfectly ideal way to live, so much easier, so beautifully carefree, so much more restful on those comfortable wheels of security. We had always just drifted with the current and we never knew where it would lead us, if anywhere. Mostly nowhere.

This way of life was all right for a time but later it became dangerously near to decadence, not bothering about work of any kind, not making an effort to get out of drifting. Eventually one becomes hypnotized, incapable of movement. And, at this point, there is the deadly arrival of authentic uncaring decadence.

The current on which we drifted later on was laced with artists and alcohol, a killer combination. Brigit escaped this rot because Brigit was Brigit, all of a rock-piece. She did not have to learn the hard way as I did. She had her values straight at the start and she stuck to them like glue. She knew what was what and she kept all her hoarded-up wisdom to herself. She was as inscrutable as a sphinx, as immutable as a pyramid. She was not subject to ordinary human weaknesses such as envy, jealousy, spite or maliciousness with which I was overflowing. Brigit could do very well without them. I could never make up my mind whether she was truly good or whether she was deliberately going through the motions of being good in order to avoid any extra unnecessary hurt, of which she had had a bellyful in her growing-up years. Whether she was, that is to say, too good to be true only on the surface.

But why carp and niggle about her motives if the net result is the same? My trouble has always been that I could never really believe that a person could be just plain good, born that way. In my Doubting Thomas mind, I always suspected that it must be a put-on job. Judging by myself again, no doubt!

This insecurity and isolation that both Brigit and I suffered from is one very good reason that the P.N.E.U. school was such a godsend to us, such a beneficial release from the stifling trap of artists and alcohol that threatened to engulf us. And, in my case, disastrously did. Our lack of formal education also left us with a long list of things we did not know. And that ignorance may explain why in later life we all felt the need to fall back on nature as the only subject we knew, although, in point of fact, we knew so little about it. We simply lived, in crass ignorance, in it.

I can just imagine, at this point, my two sisters responding indignantly: speak for yourself! And, it is true, they took in a lot more than I did. Nicolette, later on, did make a serious study of birds' eggs and even got a job in the British Museum in London putting in chronological order the confusion of valuable eggs left there from way back. That impressed Brigit and me enormously, especially the fact that she was paid for it!

Then she had the really remarkable courage to take off on her own, with a lump sum from somewhere, in a pack of keen birdwatchers, to Iceland and St. Kilda of all places in search of the very rare black eggs. These were the same black eggs she wrote about in her book of that title.

Brigit and I were left agape at Nicolette's escapade. I, of course, was purple with envy... while the Blessed Brigit had no envy in her. We both stood in awe of Nicolette for her sophistication, her ambition and her adventurousness. We called her efficient way of getting what she wanted her "French side," which was both a compliment for her clever efficiency and a disparagement of the calculated materialism associated with it.

Brigit also loved nature. She knew intimately all the devious paths and byways through or round the clumped woods. She had a nose for smelling out the right direction. It was like magic to me. I always got into a panic when I was too far from home in the middle of a wilderness stretching in every direction to infinity. But not Brigit. She calmly took her bearings, then turned unerringly, like the horses under us pulling forcibly back towards their stables, towards house and home.

Brigit was an expert, too, at looking after horses, though when and how she learned to do all these skilled jobs, I haven't a clue. She pried open their long, yellow-toothed mouths and dosed them with a huge black cylindrical pill. She washed their lower quarters with a huge sponge, then rinsed them off with the hose. Most of the horses obviously enjoyed this procedure, but the nervous ones jumped with fright and kicked out at her. She cleaned out their stables in the mornings like a man and laid down sweet-smelling straw for them.

I shall never forget the delicious bran mashes that Brigit made for the horses on the winter evenings when their chests were wheezing with common colds. She mixed the bran with boiling water and great wooden spoonfuls of Lyle's Golden Syrup which, when she had strenuously mixed it together, we greedily spooned into our own mouths. The horses' bran mash always tasted so much better, we thought, than the dull stuff we got for supper.

Brigit was also marvellous in the kitchen garden and did all the man's work there better than a man. In fact, our old gardener, seeing how much more thorough and scrupulous she was than himself, was put out and soon retired from his job altogether. Brigit loved the feel of the earth, and she was a champion digger. Digging and turning the earth did something unfathomable for her. It was a fine therapy. And all the fresh vegetables that she had planted and grown were laid on the table: new potatoes, green peas, runner beans, French beans, broad beans and crisp salads. They tasted quite different from anything we got in the shops. Twenty times more genuine and beautiful.

Brigit had only to produce a boiled egg and bread and

butter or an apple with strips of cheese beside it for them to taste like manna from heaven! And, when I allow myself to brood over her Irish stews, her sizzling brown sausages neatly lined up in the frying pan and her baked potatoes in the oven in their crackling skins, my mouth begins to drool and I am overcome with nostalgia.

After all the racketing round and battering the hell out of myself that I have done, in the name of instructive experience, all that remains now at the end of my life is Brigit's boiled egg and her apple and cheese. It is evidently true what the psychologists say: the earliest years in an individual's life are the most significant. They are the ones that remain most clearly in the memory.

4
Bird-nesting

Among my sisters' and my many passions, in those passionate days of developing youth, was bird-nesting in the comparatively small area of countryside surrounding our home. Each of us strove to outdo the others in finding nests or birds. We never took all the eggs (only vulgarians did that); we took only one, or at most two, out of a nest of six or seven, so that the bird would not miss them and would go on sitting on its remaining eggs. If there were fewer than six eggs, we only took one, for fear the bird would notice and abandon its nest.

I would pray as I had never prayed before, going along the lanes, to be the next one to find a nest, even if it was only a common blackbird's or thrush's nest. Actually, I loved the thrush's nest lined with mud or hardening cow shit, with its four or five blue eggs shining up at the sky. It was a beautiful sight. The blackbird's nest was very drab by comparison. I had not much hope against Brigit, who always seemed to know, by instinct, where the nests were hidden. She did not hesitate to penetrate even the thickest hawthorns, where she was scratched all over but did not give a damn. Of course, the lanes with hedges were the last places for rare birds to build their nests. They would seek spots farther away from human reach; remote, inaccessible places.

Bluebell Wood was where I found my first rare bird's nest. I had seen the small brown bird creeping busily up and down the trunk of a tree, more like a mouse than a bird. Whenever we saw a likely looking tree trunk, we always carefully examined all the holes in it, thrusting our hands and arms, sometimes up to the elbows or shoulders, deep into the soggy leaves and damp tree-mush. We were in a state of great trepidation, but it had to be done; those were the rules of the game. We never knew what might be there to jump out at us or peck at us or bite us. An owl might jump out at us and claw out our eyes; or a rat, cowering in the dark, might bite off our fingers with its vicious teeth; or, worse still, there might be an unknown frightening entity that might do anything. Having probed abortively into so many holes in the trunks of trees before, with never any positive results until now, I could not believe it when I actually felt at the end of one long narrow hole a soft, feathery nest filled with tiny eggs. My excitement was intense and I was trembling all over. It was with the greatest difficulty that I managed to extricate one of the tiny eggs. It was white and speckled at the top. I had never before seen one like it and had no idea what it was. I knew only that it was a new bird for me. So I hastened to extricate one more egg the best I could. They were so tiny and delicate I was afraid they would get broken on the way home. I was in a hurry because I was dying to show my great find to my two sisters and to discover, with the help of the bird books (of which we had a stack) and Nicolette's superior knowledge, to what bird the eggs belonged. By studying all the relevant details, we unanimously pinned down our bird as a genuine tree creeper. The rare find was chalked up to me.

Then came the precarious, messy business of blowing the

eggs into a saucer. With a needle we made a tiny hole at the thin end of the egg and a slightly larger one at the fat end, in order to blow out the contents. We were never quite sure beforehand whether the eggs would be fresh, and the liquid contents blown out easily, or addled, with a fledgling bird blocking the exit. There was the test of putting the egg in a jug of water. If fresh, it sank to the bottom and if addled, if floated. But it was not an infallible test. More often than not, an egg was something in between—neither completely fresh nor completely addled—hesitating midway between the top and the bottom of the water.

We would puff and puff as though by sheer will-power we could make an object twenty times larger than the hole emerge from it. Eventually we would enlarge the hole at the fat end of the egg, and all at once, a fledgling bird would plop out into the saucer, almost invariably breaking the whole egg-shell in the process. The downstairs rooms of our house (barring our mother's sitting room, which was strictly out of bounds) were littered with saucers of mixtures stinking of rotten eggs. I cannot understand why our mother, the most fastidious of ladies about her own person, never protested, never told us to tidy up, clear up our mess.

In fact, she neglected us deplorably; she did not seem to see us or the litter surrounding us. Most children complain of being nagged too much, but we missed being nagged. It is, after all, a sign of attention, of taking notice, a sign of caring enough about the persons nagged. To our mother, we three, evidently, were not even worth nagging. Luckily we had each other upon whom to vent our excess energies; otherwise our lives would have been intolerably lonely.

We certainly could have been termed "neglected children" from the point of view of demonstrative love from our mother and formal, domestic and social education. But one can't have it both ways: the wild life side by side with the regimented life. They would eclipse each other. Are not neglected children far nicer than pampered spoilt ones? We liked to believe so, anyhow, and that was all that mattered to us. I think now in retrospect that we got more out of our neglected life than we could have got out of a schoolroom.

We got marvellous health for a start, on the detested goat's milk that our mother insisted upon giving us. And we were not dirty underneath—at least we didn't smell it in all that open air—only on top in the gypsy sense—although we were dishevelled in our rags, and most colourful rags at that. We changed our clothes twice a week and we had baths at night, all three of us together in a very small tub, standing up naked and screaming and splashing each other all over, then collapsing in the dregs of lukewarm water (most of it was on the floor) in fits of uncontrollable giggles.

Farmer Witt's fields to the right of our house, with a delicious little stream bubbling and gurgling through them, were the ideal place for bird-nesting. Countless small chattering birds, such as hedge-sparrows, linnets, chaffinches, robins, even yellow-hammers, wrens—the smallest of all birds—blue tits, long-tailed titmice and other endearing little birds, abounded along the bushy banks of the stream. The long-tailed titmouse had perhaps the most beautifully and intricately constructed nest of the lot, stuck in a nearby prickly bush for all with searching eyes to see. It was the lightest thing on earth. It swayed in the breeze and seemed in danger of being blown clean away at any moment. But no fear, the long-tailed pair knew better than that; it was firmly attached to the bush by invisible threads. It was oval-shaped and made out of all sorts of dry grasses and herbs and minute twigs skilfully woven through and coated with grey clinging lichen to hold it together. It had a tiny hole in the side for the tiny parent birds to go in and out. Inside, a mass of suffocating, soft-as-swansdown warm feathers concealed the tiniest of eggs buried underneath them. What a luxurious little boudoir!

The wren's nest, built on similar lines to that of the long-

tailed titmouse's, with a hole in its side too for an entrance
and exit, was a very poor ramshackle imitation of the luxury
penthouse of the titmouse. It was made up of old leaves and
bits and pieces of string strung together any old how, with
none of the aristocratic care and devotion lavished on the
house of the titmouse. The poor little wren was rather like an
insignificant, dowdy relation.

The cuckoo in Farmer Witt's fields never stopped cuckoo-
ing away in pure spontaneous aggression. It was debating in
which bird's nest it would lay its bastard egg. Its egg was usually much larger than the eggs already in the nest, but the
hostess bird often failed to notice the discrepancy and
hatched it along with her own brood. (If she did happen to
notice the rogue egg, she would abandon the whole nest.)
What is more, the fledgling cuckoo was far stronger than its
foster siblings and pushed the weaker ones roughly out of
their nest. It was also far greedier than them and grabbed all
the tastiest titbits brought to the nest by its overwrought,
long-suffering foster parents.

But it was the kingfisher that was the star turn, the Blue
Prince of Witt's fields, of a vivid Prussian blue that quite took
one's breath away. As it flashed across the stream I stood there
transfixed, not daring to move, not able to believe my eyes,
but it disappeared as soon as it had appeared. An exultant
desire came over me to find its hole in the bank of the stream
where it made its nest. I prayed as I had never prayed before
that I might find the kingfisher's hole.

Some days later, in a widening part of the stream where
the water collected in a deep pool, I did indeed see my kingfisher again! There was no mistaking the king, and this time
he did not disappear at once. He was intent on some business
of his own, swooping hither and thither, to and fro, above a
most auspicious-looking hole in the bank opposite me. I studied this hole avidly, trying to judge my chances of getting at it
and into it. Getting into the icy water up to my waist or neck

with all my clothes on or with none at all on was no problem
to me (we were all used to doing an instant striptease when
necessity called for it), but the hole was too high up. It was
equally inaccessible from above. From there it was too far
down. With that inborn craftiness that all birds have, my king
had found the exact spot in which to place his hole.

My determination was such that I had to find a way to get
at that hole. I could not ask either of my two sisters to help
me as that would have taken away from my own personal triumph. At the same time, I had to bear in mind that my king
was a shy bird and, if there was too much noise around his
solitary refuge, he would fly away in disgust. Of his much
more inconspicuously plumed wife I had, so far, seen nothing.

All that night I racked my brain about the best way to
tackle my dilemma. I thought of a boat, but I had not got a
boat. I thought of a raft but I did not know how to make a raft.
Eventually I was reduced to thinking of an old rickety chair in
the woodshed that I might carry along in the morning, across
Witt's fields, without attracting any attention. And this preliminary part I managed without mishap.

Then, when I got to the deep pool in the stream, I floated
the chair across the water and leaned it, upright on the stony
ground underwater, against the bank where the hole was. But
climbing on top of it, while it wobbled abominably on the
pebbles below, was not so easy.

I could feel the chair slipping from under my feet. I could
get no grip on the smooth hard sandy bank, which was without any convenient tufts of grass to hang on to. But, having
got so far, I had to go on, so I dug and burrowed frantically
into the hole facing me.

I thrust my right hand and arm along the rough gritty passage. I felt dimly, tentatively, at its far end, a kind of squelchy
gluey mixture. Whether the bird's eggs or even fledglings
were mixed up in it, I could not tell.

Involuntarily I jerked back my arm. My hand was all sticky

and gooey from the fishbone vomit of my king and, in that abrupt staccato movement, need I say what happened? The chair fell over backwards in the water, with me on top of it.

I should have laughed but I did not (I was never a great one for laughing at myself), and my pride and dignity were far too outraged. I knew I should not have given up so soon, that I should have gone back and tackled the job again in a calmer, more objective way. It was against all our pioneering principles to have made such a botched job as I had and, worse still, to have left it half done. But for once I had not the heart to go on: I had suffered a grave disillusion in my king. His indoor habits did not match his outdoor glory. I could not reconcile his two opposing sides—his romantic plumage on the outside with his squalid home on the inside. My only comfort was that my king had not been present during my ignominious performance. At least he did not witness the debacle, and I was able to preserve intact his original dashing image.

5
Ethna Smith

Ethna Smith was one of the most extraordinary and original women I have ever met. And, I think, in her strange way, one of the most wonderful. We met her first in the New Forest, where she lived all by herself in a small corrugated iron hut, next door to a small post office that sold everything. And she always kept two or three horses in some stables a little way below her hut. She was a crack horsewoman, and her whole life was concentrated down in the stables with her horses. Her hut was merely a dumping ground for the frugal needs of her body. Only in the saddle did she take on her true dignified stature. She was an extension of her horse and always looked a bit wrong, a bit awkward and odd, dismounted. She looked perfectly right and proper only mounted on top of a horse, scanning the far horizon.

Ethna Smith was tall and very thin: skeleton thin. It was impossible to imagine her out of her skin-tight riding breeches, which she seemed to be sewn into, or to imagine her peeling off the riding boots that clung to her stick-like legs.

We often wondered: did she take them off when she went to bed? And we came to the conclusion that she could not, even had she wanted to.

She had protuberant piercing crossed blue eyes with a pronounced squint. She was crowned by a tangle of fair hair that obviously had never had much to do with the simple rake of a comb. She might have imitated us as models of elegant hairdo fashion! She had a mouth twisted sideways to make people believe, we felt, she was sneering at the world in general. And yet, in spite of this mock cynicism and defiance of hers, we somehow knew instinctively that she was good inside, that she had an oversized heart ticking away, under layers and layers of wadding that she had learned to wrap it up in. But she could not deceive Brigit or me. We were old hands at this game of concealing the tucked-away heart. We recognized at once that her tough outer mask was to conceal her damnable shyness. We knew, because we both suffered all our lives from the same handicap. So we ignored the harshness of her looks and bearing and way of speaking.

We asked her all sorts of questions about all sorts of things. But it was quite impossible to draw her out about anything, especially about herself and her past life. She only grunted back at us in surly monosyllables. She came into her own only when she was giving us curt orders on how to handle and manage a horse: on all the finer meticulous rules and etiquette of learning to ride a horse correctly.

It was Ethna who taught us to ride. She was a tyrannical teacher, and it was a brutal school she put us through. Her theory was "stick the bum on the saddle or be thrown and trampled under clattering hoofs."

One of her favourite systems of getting us broken in to the unexpected shyings and caprices of our unpredictable animals was to keep her highly bred racing mare (Two Star by name) shut up in her stable for two or three days and bloated solely on oats. When, on the third day, Ethna led her out of the stable, Two Star was dancing fresh, hopping mad, bucking out with her rear legs and raring to go with her forelegs. Whereupon our gentle teacher got Two Star bridled and saddled up—tugging fiercely at the girth under her belly while Two Star circled madly round and round. Ethna then quickly hoisted up one of us terrified victims into the saddle and, without more ado, gave a resounding crack of her riding crop right on the mare's backside.

Two Star took off like a shot out of a gun. After the first spurt of pure undiluted terror—casting around frantically and vainly in my frozen mind for ways of escape—I gradually settled down to my galloping and got the message. I stopped tugging at the reins. Nothing in heaven or on earth could have stopped that crazy racing mare anyway. There was only one way of dealing with such a hopeless predicament and that was to be more brutal, if possible, than my tormentor. So I gave her her head. I kicked her sides as hard as I could with my unspurred boots. I beat with all the force of my futile hands on her undulating, sweaty haunches and withers. And, at the same time, I hissed and snarled curses and imprecations into her viciously flattened-back ears.

I actually began to enjoy this hell-bent race, to exult in the speed and the wind rushing past my face. I could not now go fast enough, I wanted to go faster and ever faster—never to stop. This was the life! Two Star's manic evil spirit had got into me. As she began eventually to slacken her pace, I would have none of it. I drove her on and on relentlessly beyond her strength. I had to make her eat the dust and drop down dead for the frightful ignominies she had put me through. "I will teach you to make a fool out of me," I gloated at her with sweet revenge, as I drove the dropping creature on.

Although Ethna Smith would sooner have died than give me a compliment or a good word, I could see by the reluctant astonishment in her dilated crossed blue eyes that she was quite impressed by my marathon feat of endurance on Two

Star, and the unbelievable fact that I had somehow stuck in the saddle through that ordeal (I was held on by suction of the air and had no choice but to stay on) and that Two Star herself had self-evidently and undeniably got the worse of that battle. Ethna Smith said nothing, of course, but neither did she pat Two Star. She led her silently back into her dank stable—Two Star was too hot then to be given water—and, this time, she was given no oats. Two Star had let Ethna Smith down. Ethna had depended on Two Star to wipe the floor with me. What a disillusion it was for her!

Ethna Smith possessed all the necessary attributes for inspiring ardent crushes upon herself from two impressionable young girls. And both Brigit and I developed just such crushes on her wild, uncouth, free spirit. We both longed to be exactly like her—without a grain of tenderness to mar our bold, brave, adventuring image. But, most of all, perhaps, we fell under her spell because she treated us like two pieces of dirt.

Fear, in the sacred equestrian school of thought, is an inadmissible quality. It is the acme of bad taste even to mention the word in connection with this worshipped animal. And yet the horse is an erratic animal with a malicious imagination all its own. It is adept at all the capricious tricks for tossing its rider off in embarrassing attitudes. It is particularly fond of wedging its head down between its nobbly knees and refusing to let it be heaved up again. Its sweating-blood rider then has no choice but to slide down its sloping-downward neck onto the ignominious ground. One never knows, before starting out on a strange mount all in one piece, whether one will return *still* all in one piece. It is, in fact, always a bit of a miracle if one does.

Brigit and I had two major, inadmissible fears. The first was of our teacher and tormentor: Ethna Smith. The second one was of the horses she perversely chose to mount us on. But of the two fears, our fear of our teacher was by far the greater.

When the season for the horse shows, gymkhanas and horse jumping came around, I always became very nervous. But I kept it a secret, of course, because I had to put up a front of keen enthusiasm. With the excuse that neither of them could bear to face the public, Ethna Smith and Brigit both quietly opted out of the test. Instead they used me as their prize example of all the skills that Ethna Smith had beaten and hammered into Brigit and me for months.

Nobody loved showing off more than I did—if it came off. The other side of me was cringing inwardly that it would not come off, that I would not succeed in doing honour to my teacher, that I would, in point of fact, make a muck of it. What it amounted to was: if I did well, all went well; I was boosting up my teacher. If, on the contrary, I did badly, all went badly; I was letting her down. It was that obligation to my teacher that took away all of what might have been my joyous spontaneity in going through, first, the comparatively easy competitions of horseback riding and then the tough jumps at the end.

The grand finale of the horse show was, inevitably and inescapably, the jumping contest. For sheer excitement, probable catastrophies and plain terror, there was nothing to beat it. The crowd came to life, sat up straight in their seats and leaned forward all agog. My heart sank into the soles of my short boots. My head rang with alarm bells. My stomach caved in and rumbled its disapprobation.

I had no confidence in myself or my horse. To be more precise, I had no confidence in the combination of the two of us together. I was riding Ethna Smith's special personal horse, Brandy. She always rode Brandy herself to perfection when out with us, but refused to ride him in public because of her pathological shyness. How could I possibly do justice to both Brandy and Ethna's expectations of our joint performance? Added to which, incredibly, I had never ridden Brandy before.

We had no previous understanding of each other, Brandy and I, no practised harmony together.

Brandy was not my type of horse. He was perfectly trained, but I was not used to such a tall horse; he was from fifteen to sixteen hands high and too aristocratic, too bony, too narrow and angular for my taste. I liked my horses compact and bouncy with a nice wide seat and a motion like a rocking-horse.

The whistle went and my number was called out. I should have confidently cantered round the ring a couple of times to warm us up, then spurred on my horse to make a dash at the first jump for a subsequent flying leap over it. But in my panic I forgot all these elementary rules. Instead of cantering, I reluctantly crept up to the first jump and stood almost stock-still in front of it. I had an idea at the back of my mind that Ethna Smith always reined in Brandy very tightly and took him dead slow up to the jumps. But I was wrong again, not for the first time, as Ethna informed me afterwards in tart tones. Fortunately for me, Brandy, with all his training behind him, took off abruptly from an almost static position.

The ultimate beauty of a jump depends mainly on the placing of one's horse neither too far away from the jump nor too near it. This placement plus an urgent forward pressure of both of the rider's heels will create exactly the right conditions for the take-off.

Instead I dropped my reins, lost my stirrups and, on landing over the far side of the jump, fell forward, sprawling, over Brandy's sharp-edged neck. I very nearly fell off my horse altogether. With the fury that comes of personal humiliation, I just barely managed to readjust myself on the saddle and pull my bits and pieces together in time to continue my ordeal. From then on, for the whole round of fearful jumps, I was merely the abject passenger, shaken and jolted by the cool efficient driver: Brandy. Brandy had autocratically taken possession of the field and consequently ignored the incompetent object balanced unsteadily atop him.

I was seething with impotent rage and mutely cursing Brandy for so mercilessly showing up my flustered, hot and bothered ineptitude. For making me look ridiculous in public, I would have cheerfully killed him on the spot. Put a bullet, a burst of bullets, through his apology of a brain. Who did he think he was anyhow? Lording it all over the shop with his snooty superiority!

I am one of those people who, if everything goes wrong at the start, feels honour-bound, as a desperate gesture of defiance, to go from bad to worse. I cannot explain this compulsion, but I think I feel that by piling on my clownish clumsiness, exaggerating my absurd mistakes, I am taking the sting from my shaming actions. By emphasizing them more, I am deliberately making them more acceptably amusing. Anything is better than the mundane shame of them.

I had been so busy concentrating on my own sufferings, in opposition to Brandy's sufferings in the ring, that I had not got a clue as to how we had actually fared—the unharmonious pair of us together—in the jumping scores. But I was pretty sure that we had made plenty of irregularities and petty mistakes, one way or another, and that these would all be, neatly and numerously, chalked up against us.

If I had been simply amazed previously when told that I had won the best-rider contest, I was now unimaginably more amazed, beyond belief, when I heard that Brandy and I had won the jumping contest. To say that I was thunderstruck is an understatement. I thought that there must have been some mix-up, some awful mistake. Only when I received, some time later, a handsome silver cup with Brandy's and my own name engraved on it did I finally believe that it was true. Apparently Brandy had made a clear round of jumps. He had not brushed off even a single one of the small sticks that were lined along the tops of some of the highest jumps. Once again, I had won what was not worth winning because it was not I who had won it, but Brandy. I have never enjoyed playing second fiddle and can never decide, even now, whether it is preferable to play second fiddle or to have no fiddle at all. In any case, I have finally committed myself to having no fiddle at all to play—but able to call my soul my own.

When I saw Ethna Smith again, after my display on Brandy, she had only one question to ask me: "Why did you not quicken up your pace before take-off at the jumps?" I did not because I thought wrongly that she did not and I was trying to be as like her as I possibly could. A fatal thing to do, doomed to failure. An imitation of another person has no guts in it. Better to be oneself with all one's faults than a weak imitation of a strong person.

But it was useless to answer her; she would not have listened to me. I could never have got a word in edgeways through her impenetrable crust. Dear Ethna Smith. How devotedly Brigit and I loved her!

One ill-fated day, many long years after the seasons of horse shows and gymkhanas—or of the ascendancy of Ethna Smith—a nondescript man called at our front door wanting to buy any silver or gold objects in our possession. Being, as usual, stony broke ourselves and not having anything else to offer him, we collected together all our silver engraved cups of various sizes (not real silver, of course) that we had won over all the many show-riding seasons and presented them to him, asking him how much he would give us for them, if anything.

After giving them a cursory, disparagingly snooty once-over, he offered us thirty shillings for the lot. We thought this was a most generous offer: it seemed an enormous sum of money to us at that time. So we hastily agreed, handed over our armfuls of cups and snatched up his money before he could change his mind.

We considered ourselves extremely fortunate to have struck such a fabulous bargain. We even felt guilty about the poor man, who must have been out of his mind to have given us so much cash for our stupid old cups. It was only much later, in foreign climes, that I came to realize that we had sold not simply stupid old sentimental mock-silver cups, but the invaluable evidence of boasts. We fervently denied, of course, our prowess. We had perfected the fine British art of arduously fishing for compliments for some accomplishment, while simultaneously denying that we possessed one shred of talent in it. Those cups would have been solid proof of those skills we pretended not to have—and of the endless hours we spent with Ethna Smith honing them.

6

The Fields in Front of the House
with the Elms and River

Never shall I forget the solidified gloom I saw out of the misty windows in the morning, those unchangeable elm trees, the drooping strawstack and the haze of mist that covered the fields in front of the house. I have never entirely recovered from a permanent blight cast over my soul at this sight. But once we were actually in those same fields later on in the day, their whole complexion altered radically. And once we had got past those awful cows that rounded on us fiercely, staring at us inquisitively with horns cocked, a whole new world opened for us.

The River Avon was a stupendous thing for us, a truly marvellous river. Even the far fields going down to it—all squelchy and mushy and reedy and rushy—were quite different from the hard dry ones near our house. They were alive with a carpet of fat yellow buttercups and kingcups, with screeching and yelling peewits and snipe whirling above our heads to distract our attention from their mottled eggs camouflaged on the bare stony ground.

Ours was not a wide river. In fact, it was narrow and, for that reason, was extremely fast with a powerful and dangerous current that carried us helplessly towards the town and the dam where the salmon leapt. The great thing was not to fight it, not to struggle against the current, not to try to swim back up it. That way lay disaster. It would only have exhausted us, worn us out uselessly. Instead we let ourselves go and allowed the current to have its head. We let it push us along in its icy grip at lightning speed, and joyfully surrendered to it. Gradually, we crossed over diagonally to the far bank. There, starkers as usual—I don't think we possessed any bathing suits—we pulled ourselves out like so many dripping and shaking dogs, our long hair straggling down our backs, wonderfully invigorated. On that far side of the river was sacred, strictly forbidden territory. There was an abundance of protected bird-life there. A glut of pheasants and partridges innocently awaited the shooting season. When the time came to shoot them, they were so lazy and fat that they toppled into the laps of the bold huntsmen.

On our side of the river there was also private property, of course, but it was not so jealously preserved because there was no protected bird-life there. Far fewer pheasants and partridges flew freely in our woods. The cock pheasants occasionally let out a raucous scream as they took off indignantly from the cover of the undergrowth—their beautiful long tails rocketing orange and gold up into the sky—at the sound of our tramping feet crackling under the trees. Or, worse still, at the sight of our nosy dog sniffing and burrowing frantically into the rabbit holes under the bushes.

On our arrival at the far side of the river, our initial fear was that the keeper, an old familiar enemy of ours from the past, would descend on us and bawl us out. Sure enough, he spotted us right away and came blundering furiously through the reeds and rushes, all red in the face and puffing.

He started off righteously blustering at us but found himself slightly at a disadvantage when confronted by a row of three undraped females of almost nubile proportions staring at him stupidly and putting on a mock-innocent act. It was very useful, this dumb act of ours, and, frankly, often very near the truth. After expressions of disgust and contempt for both our indelicate immodesty and our continued impenitent breaking of the laws of the land, the keeper turned tail and fumbled his way backstage. We felt that we had won that first round and could get on now, fairly peaceably, with our exploration of this new exciting territory.

On our return journey, we had to again fling ourselves into the river and manoeuvre back to where our little piles of flung-off clothing were waiting for us. No danger of anybody stealing them.

We walked home feeling beautifully relaxed and full of well-being. It was the cocktail hour for the loudly cawing, gossiping and shouting rooks that congregated in the tops of the tall trees. It was embarrassingly similar to human behaviour, but the rooks had no booze to excuse their exuberance. Then, a short time later, at an unseen signal, the rooks abruptly packed up and silently flew away in straggling black strings into the night—to God knows where. There was something oppressive, something that spoke of doom in those departing rooks.

Among the tall trees in the woods monopolized by the rooks there stood one tree set distinctly apart, an extra-long, extra-thin, extra-slimy one, with a naked, branchless, unscalable trunk that led up to a solitary roofed stick nest at the very summit. It belonged to none other than the stealing magpie. I was dead keen to look inside that nest, to see all its stolen treasures, and I tried to think of every possible means by which I might gain admission to it. But by placing the nest in the remotest position, swinging in the fragile upper branches of its slippery tree, with no strongholds or footholds up to it, that crafty bird had made certain sure that nobody was going to get at its precious treasure trove.

I could not bear to admit defeat, so great was my longing to look at all the magpie's little shining trinkets. I have to admit that I yearned to pinch from that pinching bird something for my personal decoration! (No limit to vanity, no doubt about that, but it is also what keeps me going.) I could never believe that if I wanted a thing badly enough I could not have it. That was a lesson that came very hard to me and took a very long time to sink in. It was the same when I gazed in shopfronts and saw some piece of apparel only a few inches behind the glass that I absolutely *must* have. It was obviously made for me, and would have transformed my whole person into something magical. I could never accept the unpalatable fact that merely because I had not enough miserable coins in my possession I could not have the article of my fancy. It was not logical, it did not make sense. The thing that galled me most, I think, about that stealing magpie gloating at me, up there in its tree-top, was that it was cleverer than I was and had outwitted me. Whether I liked it or not, I could not deny the disgrace that I had failed to see inside its greenly envied nest. And even now, fifty years distant from that frustrating day, I still regret it.

It was when we got to the last fields of all, the ones in front of our house with the gloomy elms and the drooping strawstack in them, that we noticed the carthorses that had been let out to grass after their day's work. We had always loved carthorses and gazed with amazement and delight at their enormous hairy hoofs, their dishevelled shaggy manes and tails, their unbelievably broad armchair backs, and their general good-natured lovableness.

Without saying a word, I took a run, as I had seen done in cowboy films, and vaulted, with a great heave, onto the bare back of one of these mountainous carthorses. I noticed then that Brigit had followed suit and was already seated, straddled bareback, on another one. The carthorses felt extraordinarily large and comfortable after the slim riding horses whose backbones cut into one like knives. These horses were solid as rocks and as immovable, already worn out and weary from their hard day's work, so they had no intention in the world of moving again for us. But we had no pity for them and were equally determined to make them move. We kicked their fat sides frantically with our sharp heels and lashed out at their huge rumps with supple switches. At last they began to lumber clumsily round the fields, then to pick up their hoofs as they gained momentum and, finally, to tear like tanks at full speed round the fields. The other unmounted carthorses, looking on at our wild circus, decided to join in and bolted after us in a stampede. Our chosen carthorses naturally had no bridles on, so there was no way of stopping them by pulling with the reins at the bits in their mouths, nor had they even, most probably, been ridden before. They were not susceptible to the spoken horse words and tones of voice to which trained horses respond. All we could do was to hang on to their manes and wait and pray until they slowed down and gave up. .

There comes a moment when the first fear and dread are transformed into delicious delight. One must simply get beyond fear or, if you like, above fear. It is simply a question of switching roles: if one's pretentious animal is terrifying one, one must terrify one's pretentious animal. It can be done. Lose fear and one automatically gains mastery. There is nothing more to lose because one does not care any more what happens to one, and not caring is an unbeatable weapon. Even if one is not completely convinced of one's own fearlessness and mastery of the situation, it must be convincingly faked, so that one's perverse beast is thoroughly convinced of it and will consequently be flummoxed and fold up.

This tactic takes the wind out of the beast's sails. It realizes that it is no longer master of the situation and that its new master, now seated squarely on its back calmly controlling the situation, is infinitely stronger than itself. There is no fun any more for the poor, now-beaten-down beast in terrifying the victim on its back, because the positions have been reversed and it finds itself instead the terrified victim underneath its new tyrannical master!

Sad to relate, this rule holds true not only in the bestial world. It is equally efficacious in a world of different kinds of beasts.

Make no mistake, a horse—a typical horse, that is—is not an amiable lovable creature when left to its own devices. It is a bitchy vicious creature and it needs dominating. If it is not dominated, it will dominate you, and it is not nice being a worm.

Sitting up on my carthorse's broad seat, my knees stretched apart and clutched round its huge bulging belly full of grass, was a marvellous sensation. And once I had forgotten my fear, I egged mine on to greater and greater lengths of rocking motion with its enormous galloping hoofs pounding away on the ground below me. I had never felt anything so beautifully sensual before—nor since for that matter—and I longed for it to go on and on and on indefinitely. My carthorse was enjoying it as much as I was—one can always tell one's partner's real enjoyment. But, like all ecstatic experiences, it had to come to an end. So Brigit and I slid regretfully off our exhausted carthorses' backs, fearful that the irate owner would ban us from both the carthorses and the fields in front of our house. That delicious day, however, we were lucky and nobody bothered us.

7

Maurice Chevalier and Greta Garbo

Our mother believed very strongly in early to bed for her three boisterous daughters; she did not bother so much about early to rise. After twelve hours she could not have kept us in bed much longer in any case. But she omitted to take into consideration that the bedtime hour should have been made proportionately later when we were burgeoning into our teens. Or see that it was a trifle ridiculous for big hulking elephants like us, at that bulging age, to be retiring every night on the dot of nine o'clock. Going to bed with the hens! Admittedly there was nothing else to do except read the whole night through, and it was more fun to read under the bed covers with a torch, to give a semblance, at least, of forbidden fruit.

Nor can I, in all fairness, really blame our beleaguered mother for establishing her right to a brief period of private life, a natural enough desire, I suppose, as I myself discovered when my turn came to be surrounded by bouncing bawling children all the livelong day. It is an essential breathing space in which to rediscover one's lost identity and to parade as an attractive woman once again, instead of having to be a suffering symbol of eternal sacrificial motherhood, a nagging ramrod of a mother. It is much pleasanter to be the wicked child on the receiving end of these constant reproofs than to be the constantly reproving battering ram of a mother. The wicked child has all the fun and takes no notice of the nagging. The mother kicks herself for abandoning so easily her wicked girlhood.

It was thus that this regular habit of nightly retirement at nine o'clock led to troubles once again. Brigit and I were accustomed to filling in the yawning gaps of the day, and so we solved this problem in our usual inventive way: by plumbing into the unknown depths of our biological fantasies.

At that distant time, our heart-throbbing crushes of the moving screen were Maurice Chevalier and Greta Garbo. Therefore, with no preliminary discussion that I can recall, Brigit promptly became Maurice Chevalier and I, equally promptly, became Greta Garbo! What an incongruous pair we must have been—two shivering-to-death sisters in our skimpy nightgowns!

We always had our narrow wooden beds pushed up close together against the icy cold in our bedroom. So we sat bolt upright against our separate pillows and proceeded to be Maurice Chevalier and Greta Garbo talking to each other. Brigit, as Maurice Chevalier, spoke in a gruff caressing voice with a broken English accent, and I, as Greta Garbo, answered him in deep husky tones pregnant, I thought, with erotic suggestion.

I would give much to be able to remember one single word of what we said to one another, but, mercifully perhaps, the whole context has vanished behind a locked and bolted door of the subconscious that no amount of brainstorming can bore through.

We were so utterly wrapped up in the characters we were

portraying that there was nothing, literally nothing, of our real selves left. We were taken over by them completely. There came a certain moment of acute, agonizing, emotional tension between us when Greta Garbo was all of a flutter and a twitter, tottering on the brink of a precipice of surrender to Maurice Chevalier. She flopped out, swooning, on her hard little pillow, like a dying duck in a thunderstorm. And it was all done with the voice alone. It says a lot for the magnetic voice of Maurice Chevalier.

By a stroke of great good fortune for our moral salvation, the traditional taboos against sisterly incest were more powerful than the oppressive drag of the carnal flesh. But only just. It was a near thing. And the most unbelievable thing in this grotesque *mise en scène* is that we never once touched each other—not with the littlest of little fingers—which only goes to show the potency of the taboos. Had our actual identities suddenly reasserted themselves at this crucial moment of Garbo's spent resistance, we would have found ourselves in a most embarrassing position, to say the least. God knows where or how we would have ended up. It does not bear thinking about.

We played this game for quite some time until eventually it fizzled out. Maybe a real, flesh-and-blood male came along to take the place of our romantic, blown-up illusions. But all I can say is that the genuine article never could have aroused such fervent passions, such palpitations in our bursting breasts, as we did in the glamorous skins of Maurice Chevalier and Greta Garbo. And although our play-acting was distinctly farcical, it had its touching aspect too, seen from this long distance.

8

The Climbing of Trees and
Making Houses in Them

Just outside Brigit's and my bedroom window stood a very ancient yew tree where we spent a good part of our idle days. It was covered with a strangling growth of ivy, which gave us good handgrips and footholds for climbing. It was not very high, though dense with spiky foliage, and at the first big fork of thick branches, there was a most convenient flat platform. Needless to say, we could not resist this invitation to hide from prying eyes, so we set immediately to build one of our many tree houses there.

First, we made a more solid base by fixing some boards between the branches; then we carried up armfuls of straw and hay from the stables and spread them as a comfortable mattress. On top of this we put old mats, blankets and cushions to lie on and to stop the spikes and thorns from the straw and hay sticking into us. Finally, we covered ourselves with bundles of old coats and strange antiquated garments to keep the cold out. Luckily for us, we always had vast collections of old clothes from years back stashed away in various cupboards. Nothing was ever thrown out by our mother for fear that the dubious object might come in useful some rainy day, which, since it frequently was a rainy day, it invariably did. It was the new clothes that were missing from our wardrobes.

Our yew tree was situated in the garden below our window overlooking the main road, where there was a bus-stop on the route to Ringwood. If it had been strategically placed there to please us, it could not have served our purposes more beneficially. We tied sacks of small green apples and acorns to the branches of our yew tree, then, when the moment seemed propitious and the targets looked worthy of our attention, we let fly our missiles, pelting them through the air like hail, apparently from nowhere, upon the apathetically waiting, dowdy group at the bus-stop. The beauty of it was that we could see their startled faces distinctly, looking all around, bewildered, but they could not see or hear us, bursting our guts in suppressed giggles.

It was not a very high-class or original occupation, and we were really much too old—we must have been about thirteen or fourteen years old by then—for such schoolboy pranks. But, as I think I have made clear before, we were exceptionally slow developers. We had no social contacts and no social life, so there was never any hurry for us to grow up. And, in many ways, I think we had more fun that way; we managed to savour the passing moment to its dregs, instead of passing on to the more sophisticated diversions before we were ready for them and which, actually, when eventually experienced much later, turned out to be much less fun than our hilarious childish amusements.

In the pitch black of an icy winter night we got up from our hard narrow wooden beds and crept down the creaking wooden stairs in our flimsy nightgowns with a few old coats and cloaks wrapped tightly around us. Braving our constant fear of the "White Lady" pouncing out on us from every corner, we unlocked the squeaking front door and in our bare feet followed the gravel path to our brooding yew tree. Once there, we dutifully climbed up it to partake of our obligatory Midnight Feast. It was the thing to do, we thought. Did not all schoolgirls worth their mettle do it in their dormitories at midnight—defying the spying night-guardians of their virtue? And since the very words "boarding school" represented to us something unattainably desirable and super-glamorous, we could do no less.

I may add that after being introduced, some time later, to the undying fascination of Dracula, our rather pathetic "White Lady" faded rapidly into the background—never to haunt us again. How could she possibly compete with such a rival as an entombed corpse who rises and takes wing at night; who crawls up the walls of crumbling mansions and flies into the open windows of expectantly waiting ladies to sink his rapier-long eye-teeth into the sides of their lily-white necks, ready-exposed, in order to replenish his dry veins on the fresh blood of live persons? And how his swooning victims appeared to enjoy it! No doubt about it, Dracula is tops in horror value and, to this day, no more thrilling, evocatory fabrication has superseded him. He has created a horror very closely and thrillingly allied to pleasure—terror and pleasure combined in an emotional feast. Who would ask for more than half a dead man and half a live vampire bat smothering them into oblivion?

We spread out on our damp makeshift bed in our night tree a sumptuous hoard of goodies which we had saved from days past, eking out our skimpy pennies.

1) Boiled sweets: hard, sticky, of various colours and flavours;
2) Acid drops: white, acid and tart on the palate as lemons;
3) Pear drops: pear-shaped, prickly on the tongue and

tasting of real pear;

4) Gum drops: all gummy in the mouth and sticking to the teeth;

5) Sharp's toffees: best make, paper-wrapped, of perfect consistency—neither too hard nor too soft;

6) Fry's cream bars: plain chocolate with scrumptious cream filling;

7) Milk chocolate "flake" bars: pure flaking heaven;

8) Milk chocolate "crunchy" bars: pure crunching heaven;

9) Liquorice all sorts: a delectable mixture of diverse liquorice-based shapes and pieces;

10) Dolly mixtures: tiny, hard, bright fragments for dolls that we swallowed in handfuls;

11) "Hundreds and thousands": minute varicoloured particles that we simply poured down our ever-open throats;

12) Turkish delight: large powdered squares of jelly-like consistency melting voluptuously in the mouth;

13) Marshmallows: the poor man's turkish delight;

14) Jelly babies: made of some sort of rubbery stuff—just like chewing up real little human babies. Compulsive chewing, impossible to stop until all finished;

15) Lollipops: we were not so keen on such babyish things and they took much too long to suck down to nought—to a thin prick of colour;

16) Bull's eyes: black-striped with a strong peppermint flavour, too strong for us;

17) Peppermint lumps: perfect peppermint-flavoured, squelching creamy cushions of yumminess;

18) Sherbet powder in cardboard tubes: we dipped in the tips of our tongues to make it froth and tickle us. Or we filled our mouths and blew it, frothing and foaming, through our noses...like angry dragons;

19) Whipped cream walnuts: walnut-shaped chocolate

with an actual walnut embedded in the chocolate at the bottom underneath all the whipped cream on top of it that, when one bit into the chocolate, came oozing out and trickling down one's chin…I did not like nuts in chocolate so I left the walnut at the bottom;

20) Halfpenny wafers: so humble sounding, but in these wafers—now unobtainable, incredibly cheap even then—resided a particular special kind of magic that no words can do justice to. We always saved them up to the last as the *pièce de resistance*…merely to think of them, years later, brings on a fit of yearning childhood nostalgia and a doubt that they ever really existed.…Only Brigit and I, who have sampled and savoured the relish and ecstasy of the halfpenny wafers, can swear to that.

This sumptuous hoard of ours was washed down with colourless fizzy lemonade, and the miracle of it was that with our iron-clad stomachs we never got indigestion. We did not know what indigestion was. And if one does not know what a thing is, it does not occur to one to have it.

9
Brigit's Pig

We were always surrounded by animals at home but, strangely enough, I can remember no dogs. It was all cats curled up
on every chair and sofa available or flung on the floor like
hairy doormats. Cats and women all over the place but no
men. It was an excessively catty combination, and it was there
I learned to make my catty remarks. Only very rarely did a
man enter our house, and then he was seen to be very ill at
ease and never stayed long.

Outside in the yard behind our house and in the ramshackle broken-down outhouses, among the ponies and
goats, there were also chickens and ducks running loose and,
most surprisingly, a tiny pink baby pig! This pig had been
transported all the way from Ireland by my middle sister,
Brigit. All alone, she held it tight on her knees across the sea
on the boat and then on the prodigiously long journey on the
train to our place. And, she told us, it never stopped its high-
pitched squealing for a second! This extraordinary feat of
endurance on her part—not to mention that of the other

passengers present—will indicate, to a small extent, the force
of Brigit's character. She was our tower of strength and our
anchor.

Anybody who thought they were somebody, and were
dolled up to kill to prove it, paled beside Brigit's overpowering genuineness, whose presence alone put all their pretences
in the shade. She was uncompromisingly herself, as so few
people have the courage to be. Our father's portrait, by
Augustus John, in the National Gallery in London is labelled
simply, "A Professional Eccentric." Brigit is the same
unadorned clay.

But our father was not our real father in that he did not
live under our roof. He left my mother when I was still a
child, and I can barely recall the sight of him on his very occasional and rapid visits to our humble home. However, we did
have a very real and permanent father—a substitute father—
in the shape of a woman friend of my mother's. We never
thought it odd then that a woman instead of a man presided
over us. She had a very strong personality and a very strong
influence over us, and our mother was putty in her hands. She
never appeared to take the slightest notice of our existence,
although strong waves of dislike emanated from her in our
direction, making me feel both invisible and utterly superfluous. Her dislike of us was returned in fearsome force. We
called her among ourselves the "Black Woman" and thought
of her as an evil being who had stolen our mother from us.
She was rich too, which added to her blackmailing power over
our mother and, like nearly all rich people, she was fundamentally mean. If rich people were not fundamentally mean,
they would not stay rich long. She distributed her calculated
favours, like inviting us to her gloomy house every now and
then, producing lavish meals served by her staff which we
overate greedily, and letting us sleep, all three girls together,
in a sumptuous triple bed where we whispered and giggled,
and tore up and down the passages in our nightgowns and

bare feet. Then we gazed out the window of our dark room, all bunched up together, on the overflow of partying grown-ups on the lighted-up lawn. Sometimes we saw a man and a woman clasped together embracing each other passionately. This free display of unmentionable lust sent delicious tremors and tinglings of mysterious excitement down our spines.

Once, to our shocked surprise and amazed excitement, we recognized the woman in the man's clasp as our very own demure French governess! We could hardly believe it and were thrilled to death. With what mocking scoffing eyes would we regard her transformation, all dignity lost, on the morrow at our lessons! But to our deep disappointment she had not changed in the least. She was just as dull and ordinary as she had always been. We could not understand it at all. What had happened to our seductive siren of the night before? How could she be one and the same person, with that maddening bland face of hers, after we had seen what she was up to? It was like a slap in the face to us poor fools. But we had not allowed for the melting processes of alcohol, nor did we even know about them at that time. Although we were none of us so very young, all in our early teens, we were incredibly green regarding the falsities of the world. Except perhaps for Nicolette, our eldest sister, whom Brigit and I regarded as the cream of sophistication after she had been to a finishing school in Paris. But, even if she had any inside intimate knowledge, any inkling of what was going on, she most certainly was not going to divulge it to us two, whom she still considered silly children. She was a very secretive girl, different from us, and it is my bet that though she liked to put on airs of hidden wisdom, she was not all that much wiser than we were—not in those days at least, when we were peeping out of a window at our first glimpse of the frightening mystery of sex—and drunken sex at that!

However, let me return now to the antics of our darling

baby pink pig, who was not to remain the family's darling for much longer. It grew at an alarming rate and became positively ferocious, even dangerous, attacking tradesmen who came to the back door. After encountering our fearsome pig a few times they came there no more. And it not only attacked strangers; it also, to our great dismay, charged at us children too—its would-be benefactors! It had a most disagreeable disposition, and we became increasingly nervous of approaching the cantankerous creature. Of course, it should have been closed up in a pigsty, but we never considered such a solution. We thought it would have been much too cruel to inhibit its exuberant freedom.

Finally our mother decided it had gone too far. The pig had exceeded all the limits and was growing larger and more belligerent every day. So she arranged privately to have it taken away in a van to be slaughtered by the butcher. When we saw the next day that our menace had disappeared, our indignation with our mother for her dastardly act was mixed, it must be admitted, with a certain amount of relief. We did, however, fervently swear that we would never, never, *never* eat the flesh of our precious pet; it would be like eating a human friend!

Some time later, however, we had pork for lunch, and most delicious and succulent it was. It never ever occurred to us dimwits then that, after such a long time had passed, it could have had anything to do with a relation of ours. But, in those days, not everybody had a refrigerator. We certainly didn't. As a result, we were ignorant of a refrigerator's meat-preserving functions in the butcher's shop; it was a classic case of ignorance being bliss—succulent piggy bliss!

10
Ethna Smith's Transformation

Ethna Smith's life had not been a happy one because she was not born a happy person. Some people are born happy and jolly and some are not, just as some people are born sad and reflective and some are not.

Strait-laced, inhibited, hidebound, bigoted as she was in her narrow mind, she was due for a fantastic transformation which, to Brigit and myself, came as a horrible shock. Overnight, it seemed, she changed from a neuter sex, encased eternally in her skin-tight breeches and boots, into a fledgling woman making her way hesitantly out of her egg-shell. It was a rude awakening for her. For us it was an alarming disillusionment.

It was all the fault of our brother, John, who came back home periodically from the Royal Navy and made it his solemn duty on each and every visit to allay the sexual frustrations of one and all of our diverse French governesses. They were only too pleased to accept his thoughtful attentions and to relieve themselves of their excess of bottled-up fervours and fermentations.

But who could ever have imagined that Ethna Smith, our private paragon of perfect unattainability, would join this sordid category of women? Yet there was no getting away from it; she had unmistakably entered into the running with our French governesses with all the impetuosity that goes with making up for lost time. Like all self-respecting up-to-date Casanovas, John possessed a smart and open racing car to facilitate his prospects with his fancy ladies. It was an irresistible bait to stupid common little women.

John always liked his women common (as our mother called them) and very neat and tiny, perhaps because his three galumphing sisters were too big for him, in more ways than one. But Ethna Smith was anything but common, neat or tiny; she was an extra-skinny galumphing giraffe. Yet there she was—a notable exception.

Thus, Brigit and I found ourselves squeezed unwillingly into the back of the car, our eyes on stalks, gimleted into the back of the head of our own dear Ethna Smith, who sat contentedly in the front seat beside our brother. It was a pain, a searing pain that tore into our bleeding vitals. Ethna was positively preening herself, trying desperately to make herself alluringly feminine. Her granite rock face broke up into crooked-toothed, beguiling smiles and, unbelievably, into funny laughing shapes. Ethna Smith laughing! It was not possible. It was a paradox; a contradiction of the constriction into which Ethna Smith, with iron will, had forced her nature. Poor Ethna Smith. She was like one of the wooden dolls we loved so much suddenly electrified into staccato animation with her flashing blue crossed eyes swivelling up sideways every now and then, surreptitiously glancing up at our brother and filled with a child's wonder. It was too pathetic. It was not decent.

They had provided for themselves, the two of them, all the proverbial props supposedly conducive to romance: music on the car radio, puffing smokes, frequent nips of spirits; dimmed lights and roaring speed through the black starry night. These assuredly created the required intimate atmosphere, the giggling chit-chats, the mysterious innuendoes, the secret understanding; in short, all the spellbound nonsense that makes people in love do what they would never do in their normal senses.

John, in his Don Juan act, was deliberately building up to a flagrant violation of a bolted-door virgin. He was courting Ethna Smith with all the frills, laying on the jam with a trowel, and she was dizzily, deliriously, licking it all up out of his treacherous hands.

Ethna Smith was still in her riding togs in the car, thank heavens. She had that much decency left. She had not yet got to the point (nor ever did) of acquiring a skirt as the final symbol of her transformation into a woman. And, I suspect that, had she had the temerity to do so, such a travesty of her masculine character would have killed the romance stone dead.

John was nobody's fool. He genuinely and thoroughly appreciated the value of Ethna Smith. He recognized that she was a very special, a very wonderful person, unlike any other woman that he had ever possessed before. And curiosity alone is an irresistible bait!

Later on, in the privacy of the night in our bedroom, Brigit and I tried very hard to imagine our brother ripping off Ethna Smith's skin-tight breeches and boots and laying her out "starkers"—her cocooned, lily-white, skinny body twitching with fright—on the iron bedstead in her rattling and squeaking tin hut in the forest. Our imaginations boggled! But of one thing we could be certain: John was a craftsman who knew all the ins and outs of his trade, so he could not fail to make it; to do what had to be done, come hell or high water. For a reputable Don Juan it was a point of honour. What, we wondered, would happen to Ethna Smith when our brother left her without a qualm to go back to the Royal

Navy? How could she resume her former identity? That was what worried us stiff!

Then one morning there was a tapping outside my bedroom window. It was Ethna Smith. I could tell she was dying to tell me all about her reactions to our beautiful brother John's overtures. But her emotions were hermetically sealed to me. Her trembling diffidence and her child's wonder were too difficult for her to convey.

After that Ethna Smith faded out of our orbit as though she had never been in it. The last we heard of her, through vague acquaintances, she had settled in Peterborough and had become an advanced alcoholic, which tardily explains how she passed her lonely evenings in her hut in the forest.

We never saw her again, but we never forgot her. My lasting vision of Ethna Smith is of her, stiff-backed, astride Brandy with her square bony shoulders, one a little higher than the other, slightly askew, receding into the far misty horizon, as they do in old films. My heart melts again for her in a pool of compassion. She was one of us! One of the solitaries, one of the lost, one of the outcasts, one of the untouchables ringing their little bells to warn all and sundry to keep out of their passage. She belonged, like us, to that great anonymous unsung multitude of the drop-outs and the dispossessed. We came from the same "family" as hers, and that is why we clung to her so loyally, for family warmth. We smelled inside her gritty, gravelly exterior all the raw innocence, all the surging desires and aspirations that were also lodged, deep below the surface, in ourselves, waiting to be snuffed out by the crashing-down ordinariness of the everyday business of living. Although one weak half of us longed for the protection and the mollycoddling of polite society, the other stronger half of us had no use for it, and preferred to retain the freedom of being the way we were, wandering alone aimlessly in our wilderness.

Caitlin, age 14, during the Ethna Smith period

*Caitlin, age 16, after a showjumping competition
at Ringwood*

*On the banks of the
River Avon, Hampshire*

Caitlin, age 17, at Ringwood
Photo by Nora Summers

Portrait by Augustus John
National Museum and Gallery, Cardiff. © Julius E. White

Flat-hunting in London in the 1930s

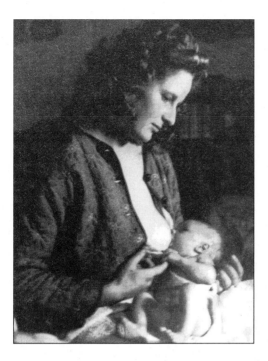

Caitlin with her first child, Llewelyn, in 1939

Dylan and Caitlin at Blashford

On the way to Puck Fair, Killorglin, County Kerry

Dylan in his element—at the White Horse Inn,
New York, 1952

Caitlin and Llewelyn after visiting Dylan's mother at Laugharne, 1958

Caitlin and her daughter Aeron on the island of Procida, near Capri, 1956

With Colm in Venice, c. *1960*

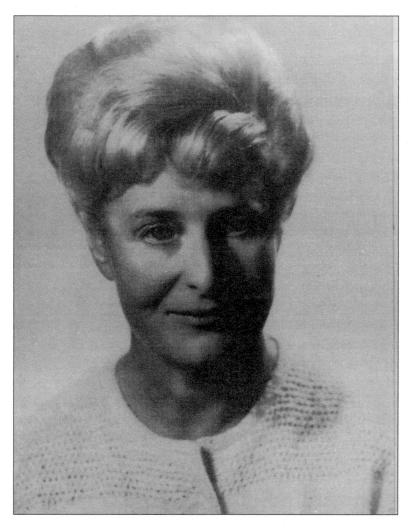

Caitlin, age 49, soon after Francesco's birth, in Rome

At the Rome zoo with a lion cub,
in the 1960s

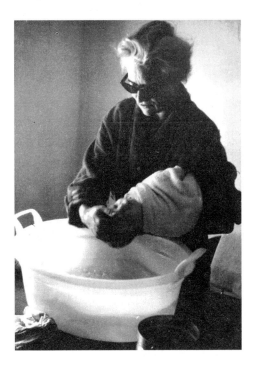

above: Caitlin bathes her youngest son, Francesco
below: Caitlin, Francesco and Giuseppe

Caitlin and Francesco in Rome

Caitlin rediscovers serenity with nature in Catania

Caitlin and Francesco in Sicily

In her Rome flat at Lungotevere, 1974

dylan

11

The Emerald Isle

When I first went back to Ireland as a young green girl (I had been there as a small child but remembered nothing of it), a most extraordinary feeling came over me: I felt I was coming home. I had never any particular feeling, one way or the other, for England, the country I was living in, but when I first went to our home at Ennistymon, County Clare, I felt uplifted; a wild lust for this country surged up in me. I felt that it was mine, that it belonged to me, that the very air of it ran singing in my veins, that it was me. I understood all of a sudden what being patriotic meant. I would have gladly died, then and there, for this green enchanted island that was in all parts of me, that was my spiritual mother. The very air of it, the very smells of it, the very stone walls of it, the very craggy roads that always went over the hill to the sea (they had nowhere else to go): they all intoxicated me. I wanted to eat them all up; to chew up the past ruminantly, like a cow. Then there was the rain, the constant refreshing rain that quenched the thirst of the spirit. Water on the outside was soothing to the spirit (it was only water taken internally that was such a damper). Rain outside, beating on the roof of the warm inside; that was delicious manna to the soul. The rain in Ireland was all part of the giant sadness already lying latent in me as a young girl. I was madly in love at first sight with Ireland in the rain. I was infatuated, I was happy. I could not believe it, but I was.

It did not last, of course. I knew, even then, that this unnatural happiness could not last. I knew I would have to plunge back, sooner or late, into real gritty life. I knew it was a glimpse, a tiny taste of paradise that would never come back again. This quickly passing possibility of a paradise on earth happened to me again when I went back to England and met Dylan, in a pub, of course, and knowingly started to drink.

How was I to know, in my unknowingness, that Ireland was the perfect breeding-ground for drunks? It had the perfect wet climate, the perfect nostalgic backdrop, the perfect poor, workless, infinitely dreary conditions for breeding drunks. How was I to know, in my unknowingness, that I too, in later years, would join their long lamentable ranks? That it was all part of the infernally romantic heritage? How was I to know that I, too, would become a typical Irish fighting drunk, born and bred? Not a very ladylike thing to become, yet an undeniable fact that I, too, in destructive time, would be smitten by the Irish sickness.

Unpredictable fate so willed that (on April 12, 1936) I met Dylan Marlais Thomas in a London pub called the Wheat-sheaf in Fitzrovia. He was far from being a rich man, let alone a duke as my mother had predicted for me. He was simply a young, very promising, but penniless Welsh poet. I don't know what it was that attracted me to Dylan at the start. It could not have been his looks; he was the opposite of my type. My type was conventionally tall, dark and handsome and, above all, silent. In mysterious silence my ideal man held me spellbound. What pregnant thoughts his beautiful black head held were best left to the imagination. Had he opened his wisely sealed lips it might have proved fatal—shattering my girlish romancing. Whereas Dylan never stopped talking. Talking was like breathing to him, as it is to most gabbling gossiping Welshwomen—a trait he no doubt inherited from his Welsh mother. This very human side of him provided his gregariousness, his social charm, his nonstop conversation about anything and everything. He came to life only when he started to talk. But I can't remember him before he started.

It could not have been Dylan's poetry that attracted me to him, for I had never read a word of it and did not try to. Poems were an agonizing toil to listen to. It was not his endless muffled gabble, for I did not follow a word of it.

As for his looks, would I really take on someone (I never quite thought of him as a man) who looked as funny as he did? He had a pink blubbery face with pop-eyes, a blob nose and loose lips, a mop of childish mouse curls on top and a tadpole body, which blew up and down according to how much beer he put in. He was definitely beneath my standards of presentability and would do me no credit when I paraded him before my critical family, my girlfriends, or my prior cast of infinitely more alluring boyfriends. They would all surely think, "What a comedown! Can't she do any better than that?"

It must have been his little-boy-lost demeanour that attracted me to Dylan. He became my very own newborn baby. But underneath that seeming innocence and helplessness lay a hotbed of cunning and scheming. Dylan rarely did not get what he wanted. He was the disguised King of Egotists, and I was his resplendent Queen of Egotists.

Dylan and I spent our first week together sleeping at the Eiffel Tower Hotel for free; Augustus John, the painter, had a permanent account there and never knew who was or was not there. A year later, in July 1937, we were married. We then went to Bishopston in Swansea, where Dylan was living with his parents, and we spent some time there before moving to Laugharne and then on to Blashford, where my mother and Brigit lived. There I awaited the birth of my first baby.

Before I went into labour, my well-meaning "nearest and dearest" had advised me to prime myself with as much of the hard stuff as I possibly could to damp down and nullify what they called "little periodical pains." They suggested I should pass out altogether, a state I had no trouble achieving by conscientiously filling myself to the brim with whisky. But, as the pains followed faster, one on top of the other, and sharper, the potency of the drink wore off completely. To my horror, I was abruptly stone-cold sober, in the grip of my body's relentless determination to turn me inside out. Whenever the iron-fisted nurse ordered me to push down, I was dead afraid of shitting the labour bed, so I tightened up all my apertures to be on the safe side. What horrifying mistakes does threatened ignorance make? I very nearly kept my first son locked up inside me for life! After forty-nine hours of unimaginable agony, Llewelyn was born (on January 30, 1939).

Although I adored Llewelyn, I had no idea how to feed him correctly. I had two crystal balls for breasts, so enormous and hard, so painfully dying to give out their milk, that none would come out. They were too taut, the skin stretched to brittle glass, to be tapped, so they had to be bandaged in a rough cloth, tightly and lumpishly against me, for three whole days, until they subsided into palpable flesh. I was terrified, in the meanwhile, that the baby would die of thirst. Eventually, one drop at a time of thick liquid was prodded and squeezed (by iron fingers) out of the nipple and into the baby's mouth. I had never known greater joy than giving milk from my breast to my baby. I kept breast-feeding him for much too long a time, but we both enjoyed it.

There is voluntary suffering and there is involuntary suffering. I am always willing to suffer voluntarily up to a point if the end justifies the means. For instance, in childbirth, when the end is a new beautiful life bursting out of one's distended belly! No rapture can compare to this justifiable one.

This extraordinary feeling I had never felt before was of actual tangible happiness. This half-bald, wrinkled, red scrap of our joint flesh was the most beautiful thing I had ever seen in my whole wide, grinning-from-ear-to-ear world. The baby boy that Dylan called the "Mongolian monkey" was sending me crazy with unprecedented delight. It was like being in love, that lovely floating feeling, treading on air, suspended a foot above the earth.

Poor Dylan had to take a back seat, and he did not like doing that at all. It had never happened to him before. He had always been the centre of attention. But no more. Not with me anyhow. In the middle of all this euphoric baby-worshipping, Dylan, already small, became dwarfed. I had always metaphorically looked up to him before, for obvious reasons, but now, after my metamorphosis, I was looking down on him from a mountain of omnipotence. Who was that little insect creeping and crawling around my feet, far down below my mountaintop, I wondered dreamily. I felt distinctly irritated by his clumsy overbearing male presence, popping in and out of the hygienic room in my mother's house (where we went first, having no alternative then), just when he was not wanted. Not knowing what to do with himself, where to put himself, among the vast array of baby's elaborate toilet accessories laid out in neat order on the bed, for the ritual bath in the morning of the "King of Kings." And he did not even wish apparently to look at our priceless treasure, snugly tucked into its little box at the bottom of our bed. He was literally averse to looking at it. I tried my best to be compassionate, but I was never the world's greatest actress and I am afraid I left him in no doubt as to who had precedence, in that initial time of becoming a mother, in my cork-popping, bubbling-up champagne heart. When the baby was clean and fed and wrapped up like a cocoon in his mummification robes, back in his box as cosy as cosy, I would lie back at last on the welcoming pillows and listen for that primeval high-pitched wailing sound that only newborn babies make in their sleep. In their slow transition from the dark-as-pitch forest of the womb into the blinding oasis of daylight. How that distorted wail twanged at the heartstrings, one by one, of its bewitched, belonging-to-it mother. In such cleverly contrived ways, the baby assures itself of an enchanted slave, until such time that it can dispense with her. No wonder then that Dylan felt horribly left out of this crashingly boring maternity saga.

On visiting day, all the excited mothers were waiting on tenterhooks for the first visit of their husbands, now proud fathers. They not only wanted to show off their shared treasure, but, what was even more important, to show off to the other mothers their respectable husbands as the most spick-and-span, prosperous pick of the bunch. And every one of these sidling-in husbands on his first embarrassing formal visit had a shifty look about him and an undisguisable air of nervous panic that he might pick out the wrong mother by mistake. And, true enough, wives in bed under such unusually happy circumstances are quite unrecognizable. In their fluffy pink bedjackets all of them emanated precisely the same beaming pink welcome. It could just as well have been one as another.

Dylan, however, being Dylan, did not turn up at all on this auspicious occasion. I tried not to mind, but I did mind all the same: I was the only mother with no husband to show for it. All I was left with was the other mothers' sidelong pitying glances that automatically concluded that I possessed no such thing as a husband to put on display with the rest of them. Only much later, long after the other husbands had been put through the other mothers' pitiless scrutiny, only later—out of visiting hours perforce, thus unwittingly focusing upon himself extra-minute attention from a multitude of piercing eyes, just at that disorderly, behind-the-screens-bedpan time—in shuffled Dylan. In somebody's much-too-long dressing gown (he never had such a luxury of his own) and flip-flapping slippers. All rumpled and disgruntled from head to foot, after a blacked-out week of drink and dissipation, with his bloodshot-now-with-guilt eyes innocently popping as usual. In spite of his bleary-eyed condition, eyes streaked with recent nightmares, Dylan had no more difficulty than a homing pigeon in recognizing me right away, although at that distressing point I was, I must confess, more than a little loath to recognize him. His purpose, it seemed, was to pull me down again, off my reigning pinnacle. His odd freakishness stuck out so much more forcibly and offensively at this late hour.

I was hard put indeed to explain to them what an important person Dylan was: our leading modern poet, our best, in fact, leading modern poet. Yes, they agreed absently and patronizingly, as though patting an over-bumptious child on the head, while wondering from what gutter I had fished that bum. They wouldn't have been seen dead walking down the street with him.

As a matter of fact, to be scrupulously frank, it did take a bit of doing to be seen walking down the street with Dylan. At the beginning, I had suffered discreditable twinges of wanting the ground to open and swallow me up. But with the steady whittling-down of time, I had got hardened to it, most likely as a consequence of Dylan's growing importance, and my growing unimportance. God forbid that I should have known it then: my own importance was the foundation of sand upon which I built all my mythical castles.

But those lucky unchosen cows knew nothing of the romance of poverty, knew nothing of the imperative perversity, the inspiring squalor of the artistic world. They were still out-dazzling each other with material possessions. Here I have got to admit, too, to be plebeianly practical, that I also could have done with a few of the convenient commodities, at least the bare essentials, from their cheap dazzlement of material possessions. I was terrified at the thought of the abominable mess and havoc of dead bottles and dead butts—made by Dylan in my absence—that I would find on going back home. I knew with terrible foreboding there would be not even one clean space upon which I could lay my Immaculate Conception. He was doomed to remain forever in my arms as I tried vainly—handicapped as I was—to create order out of chaos.

For two growing-up people a lack of unnecessary material possessions can even be a great benefit. Dreaming of what they might have, should that material lump suddenly drop out of a grey sky, is a greater pleasure than holding it in their hesitating hands and dealing with it sensibly. They are convincingly told this by those already in possession of this infamous lump who are holding on to it for grim death. But for two grown-up people, augmented by a baby, the lack of necessary material possessions can only be a great disaster. A family is a conventional edifice. To develop it, conventional props must hold it up. Not only crude money, but crude money well spent, with judicious foresight. Since we possessed neither of these two indispensable assets, the family infallibly had to fall to the ground, just as, equally infallibly, the feckless members of the family sooner or later had to disperse and go their separate ways. The surprising thing about it was that we were an exceptionally united family. There was an unbreakable bond among us all—not so much of blood but of cast iron—perhaps because of our legion of faults and the legion of mistakes we made. Wrongdoing done with love made us sling together all the more tightly in our criminal isolation.

But for me there could never be another miracle quite as surprising as that first one of my firstborn son. I could never get over the miraculous metamorphosis of birth: by going through Hell one achieves Heaven. That transcended for me by far all the rest of the emotions I had ever felt heretofore. And Dylan, crafty bugger that he was, acting virtually as my child too, managed to sneak into this sacred aura of miracles. No doubt Dylan was a "Professional Baby." He would never grow up. He had made up his mind not to. He knew exactly what he was doing. It made it a lot easier to get by that way, without too much labour. He could get away with all sorts of naughty sayings and doings, all sorts of wicked outrageous mischiefs that nobody else, because they were grown up, could ever have been permitted to perpetrate. Dylan, who had once been my one and only adored "baby," had now been superseded by a better baby, ironically given to me as a present from Dylan!

So what did he do? He did what most wronged conventional husbands would do: he drank much more than he usually did of the strong stuff. He rushed in a panic to find his latest slinky bitch, my glamorous black long-legged strapping rival from my tap and acrobatic school, from whose tough muscular flesh he had already had a couple of bites, which had evidently whetted his appetite for a second helping.

The two of them were a convincing answer to the much quoted attraction of opposites. She so hard and so black; he so fair and so soft. She could have swallowed him whole in her swarthy whale's belly. While previously she had gushed treacly sweetness all over me as her best friend—we had always loathed each other's guts—as soon as my back was turned, as soon as she saw me safely out of bounds, out of the battled sex-ring, she had snapped up my man, as a spider snaps up a fly. It was cold comfort for me to know that, with her so-much-boasted longer legs than mine, she towered above Dylan, making them an incongruously ridiculous pair to look upon. But it did help my injured pride a tiny bit, this useful element of ridicule. Dylan had always had a thing about these grotesquely tall, pea-headed, giraffe women. Presumably he wanted to compensate for his own shortness, of which he was always painfully aware. He tried so hard, in vain, to hide it with several-sizes-too-big clodhopping walking shoes, capacious hairy tweed jackets that swamped him, heightening hats on the only thing that was big about him, his weighty head. But it was all to no avail; his efforts served but to accentuate the diminutive, chicken-boned frame with its tiny fragile hands and feet that hid inside the sagging sack of his clown's disguise.

But what did I care now? I had Llewelyn. Llewelyn had Dylan's unmistakable swimming pop-eyes, only very blue, a misshaped potato of a nose and generously opulent lips. He was a caricature of Dylan.

There was a sting in the tail of my momentary near-indifference to Dylan's latest betrayal. Later on, when the baby's enchantment over me was wearing gradually thinner, it came harking back at me with redoubled force, to haunt me and twist my stomach with spasms of nausea.

I had a vision, as graphic as though I were present there watching them at it, of every intimate detail in their grotesque, because loveless, act of physical intercourse. I could plainly see Dylan's red-hot face lowering over, his bulbous snout grunting and rooting into, his slobbering lips burrowing in and sucking at the thick black spread of thatch overhanging the treacherous hatch of her cunt which usurped my proper place: opening up now, wide as a suitcase that extends inexhaustibly, that can never be packed full enough, to pack in Dylan's minnow insufficiency as easily as packing in a shoal of minnows.

It was a horrible drunken parody of Dylan's lovemaking to me. It made his lovemaking to me afterwards turn sour on me, go rotten and valueless. As soon as he touched me, that awful unforgettable vision rose up like a traitor in the box. My mind wandered off elsewhere, while my body went through the set motions—as, no doubt, did his. This is what happens unfortunately: it is the doomed fate of romantic love. Romantic love is not tenable—except in the wind.

And my own little discrepancies of fidelity in Dylan's absence never once entered into my picture of the betrayed humiliations of the martyred wife. The mind is marvellous at ignoring trifles unworthy of mention; oafs though my partners were, those incidents still counted surely, at least technically, as betrayals of the flesh.

But I knew it was no hallucination that I had seen, as I lay in my hospital bed, cradling my newborn miracle, no figment of a mind demented by jealousy. I knew it was an exact replica of what had actually happened. Dylan knew it too, though he protested far too much that he had not the palest idea of what I was talking about.

Then, as this pale idea began to get a real grip of me, could I keep quiet about it? No, I could not. Could I forget it? No, I could not. Could I hold my tongue just for once? No, I could not. Could I not diplomatically swallow down my lump of displeasure, as civilized, restrained, educated people do? No, primitively, I could not. I carped at Dylan like a fishwife, and if anything is guaranteed to kill love, carping will do it. I taunted him continually with his desecration of our holy love. But he, as continually, stubbornly and stoutly, indignantly denied all, while his pockets were carelessly stuffed with crumpled, unread or half-read love letters that left no scope for the imagination or benefit of doubt. I pored over the inner significance of every suggestive word, deliberately piling upon myself, revelling in and savouring to the acid dregs the rank bitterness of my abandoned lot.

Dylan could not even be bothered to read right through them: "Too boring," he said. He appeared perfectly unmoved, taking not a bit of notice of them, not even bothering to throw them away, tear them up or burn them, as the guilty do. He was either being devilishly subtle with me or was genuinely indifferent to them. I preferred to believe the latter, although this may not have been the case.

After the triumph of my firstborn son—but not all at once, some contemplative years later—I badly wanted a daughter next. But I was nervous too that this purely feminine element might cause disturbing ructions of rivalry, as one sees so inexplicably between mothers and daughters. However, as far as I was concerned, I need not have worried. As soon as I saw my little miniature of perfect femininity, I was in raptures. I adored Aeron, christened Aeronwy (born on March 3, 1943), unconditionally and spoilt her dreadfully.

Our third child, Colm (born on July 24, 1949), came to be known as the Golden Boy; nothing I could say would add to the positiveness of his presence. He was the only child who had more Macnamara than Thomas in him, but in spite of this drawback, he had a cornucopia of brains.

The really miraculous thing in this whole business of baby-making was that they all, without exception, turned out to be always Dylan's babies. They were incontrovertibly his: there was no mistaking them. A cursory, if deadly anxious glance at one of them on its immediate arrival, reassured me at once on this distinctly delicate point, beyond any shadow of a doubt. Its bulging browed, snub-nosed, pouting-mouthed, angelic profile could belong to no other father. Once again our suspicious unbelieving neighbours, longing for a cuckoo in the nest, had to depart with their scandalous tales between their legs.

Nobody adored and worshipped his children more than Dylan, at a drunken distance from them. But he was too much of an irresponsible child himself to be able to give them, when sober, any of the normal props generally expected from a father: sense of security, moral support or wise fatherly advice. He was not cut out for this role. For Dylan, the two roles of poet and father were in antithesis to each other. But he never interfered, in any way, with my desperate, if far from perfect, efforts at bringing up our children correctly.

When my babies started being born, there was a complete drastic revolution in my nervous system. Firstly, I could not believe that I did not want a drink at all. I mentally declined the offer of a drink. A drink would have upset and disturbed the freshness and purity of my new feeling, which I could not bear to lose. It was so marvellous in itself that it did not need a drink to make it better because it could not have been bettered. I did not even want to go to the pub at my usual appointed hour to join Dylan; but I couldn't let him down. So I joined him, so unalterable was the habit of obedience to the drinking virus, like a well-trained soldier briskly responding under military orders. And I drank as usual, in spite of it being against my new inclinations, if not more so to celebrate our propitious event, at the cost of the probability of poisoning my baby's future milk. I was also obsessed by the wonder of each of my babies. I could not believe that such a powerful emotion had invaded my individual body.

Just after the end of the war, Helen and Bill MacAlpine, our oldest friends, had the crazy idea of going to visit Ireland. It was August, the time of the age-old Puck Fair at Killorglin (in the geographical heart of Kerry), the world's oldest and longest-celebrated festival. The "King" of the fair was a large, wild male goat, known as the Puck goat, much decorated and garlanded with greenery, hoisted high above the crowds onto a covered platform where he stayed munching choice cabbages for four days and four nights. Meanwhile the populace ate and drank (the latter mostly) day and night, for the pubs were open all the four days and four nights. This was, of course, an irresistible attraction to Dylan and Bill; a challenge to be taken up. Bicycles were hired and there was great excitement and anticipation for the outing.

Bill came from Northern Ireland but I never heard a malicious or nasty word out of him, to or about anybody, and he was totally uncontaminated by all the bitter racial and religious feelings raging in his part of the country. Bill had departed from his home town a very long time ago in search of broader horizons, and had had no more connection with it. But he had retained his great native fascination and was, besides, a poet himself, which gave him one more strong point of contact and understanding with Dylan. Bill was an ideal companion for Dylan, with his remarkable gift for avoiding rows and keeping the peace and harmony flowing between Dylan and myself, which was no mean achievement. Best of all, he had a most disarming and infectious laugh, which made even me laugh—a colossal feat! He was a natural-born lovely man of whom there are, sadly, so few left.

Dylan's record for nonstop drinking standing at a bar at Puck Fair in County Kerry, drinking draught Guinness with his best friend, Bill MacAlpine, was two days and two nights: *forty-eight consecutive hours*! At the end of which time they were both still standing, exactly where they had started off forty-eight hours before. But they were only just barely standing, and looked very woebegone and sorry for themselves, not a bit like their former jaunty selves at the outset, when they boasted that they were going to stick coolly at their allotted posts for four days and four nights of solid boozing, without stirring an inch or shutting an eyelid. So, there they were, still grimly sticking, not so coolly now, to their allotted posts: a pathetic bedraggled pair of topers on their last bending-at-the-knees legs. But they were still holding fast to the bar as their last anchor of salvation in a fast sea that was fast closing over them.

They did not ride back to our lodgings on the bicycles on which they had set out so light-heartedly two days and nights before. On that third merciless dawn, their hearts were lumps of lead in their sinking bodies. They were poured, their bicycles bunged in on top of them, into the back of a van and deposited, two dead-to-the-world soaks oozing draught Guinness out of every pore, on our scrubbed white doorstep. Not even Dylan's capacity to romanticize the drab and squalid could redeem this extremely painful episode. Not even later on, with mellowing eyes, was it ever mentioned between us again.

Bill and Dylan spent the last couple of days and nights of Puck Fair unseen, unmoving and unspeaking in their penitential beds. They were unable to look at themselves, at each other or, least of all, at their crowing womenfolk, who were partaking of a hearty fried-kipper breakfast in the dining room below. They were unable to look into the nauseous face of food, or, worse still, to tolerate the nauseous stench of liquor for fear that a mere whiff would turn their overloaded stomachs in rumbling surges of unstemmable vomit.

NEVER AGAIN! They were honestly convinced this time. Never, never again would either of them ever touch another single drop of the filthy stuff, *never again*, so help them God. May they drop down dead if they did. It was the alcoholic's theme song all over again; his famous last words, while reaching for a hair of the dog that bit him. In point of fact, to give them their due, their unnatural squeamishness lasted for near-on a whole week. But they got over it by doing as they were taught to do: trying and trying over and over again. A most praiseworthy system if the means justify the end. Before our parody of a holiday was over, they were comfortably back on their black cream-topped witches' concoction.

The orgies of Puck Fair were one of the very few occasions when Dylan and Bill regretfully admitted afterwards, to their profound mortification, that the punishment exceeded the glory. I don't know which was worse: the wicked waste of our precious saved-up money or the wicked waste of Ireland's magic. Both were unpardonable.

There was nothing strange or out of the ordinary about such drinking exhibitions in Ireland. There would have been something very strange and out of the ordinary, something downright suspect in Ireland, had our menfolk not drank a drop. Though poorer than anywhere else on earth practically, a man in Ireland who did not drink was not a man. And he drank nearly always in pubs: every shop in Ireland was a potential pub, a place to drink with other men only. No women were present. This separation of the sexes and keeping-a-woman-in-her-place philosophy suited our menfolk fine, they were only too relieved to be rid of their obstreperous emancipated women.

This unwritten prohibition against women drinking in public places, with or without men, did not stop them drinking if they wanted to. And some women do want to drink as badly as men do. There is no biological difference between men and women in this respect—that is a lot of poppycock invented by men. But this prohibition makes women drink more discreetly in private, nipping in the kitchen, in the bathroom or in the back bedroom at home. And because of their guilty hurry, they lose count of how many nips they have nipped. They think they need these nips to give them a lift, even if each successive nip is pulling them farther down the well of depression. For ironically, the more depressed drink makes a victim, the more desperately she needs it. It is a depression that has become her natural irreversible habitat. She clutches onto it, as a drowning man clutches onto a rotten branch of a tree.

However, the prohibition against women drinking in public places did not apply to us, the wives of Dylan and Bill. The locals regarded us as the freak foreign womenfolk of the freak foreign menfolk to whom any number of shocking extravagances were not only permitted but revelled in, and of course profited from. We were all lumped together under the heading of the hated and mad English. The only one of us who had true-blue English blood in every one of her veins was poor unfortunate Helen, Bill's wife, who had, in addition to such ignominy, the iron nerve to confess to emerging from the unspeakable, drearily plebeian Midlands of England. It was a frightful stigma to bear through life, in the opinion of three superior Celts. It was the fashion to be any race but dead-loss English in those days. But Helen was immune to such subtle snobberies. She did not even have the sense to cook up a Russian grandmother to make herself more interestingly presentable.

Dylan was undiluted Welsh, no doubt about that, but his father, who taught the Welsh language as well as the English language, refused to let Dylan learn it as he thought, in his Welsh mind, it would detract from his making a gentleman out of him. Dylan always complained about his father's false pretensions, but he was too lazy to learn Welsh later himself, though it would have helped his prestige as a Welshman. Bill and I were mostly Irish by origin. Bill came from the small disgraceful red area of Northern Ireland which, though the people seemed as identically charming to us as those in the Free State, took a load of living down. And my father came from the fairyland of the west of Ireland, which put me on the top throne of our current snobbery. In truth, we weren't the red-hot Celts we liked to pretend to be. None of us could speak our native language, though we kept quiet on that delicate subject and, more embarrassing still, we could hardly follow a word of the famous lilting and slurring Irish brogue, which was like a foreign tongue to us. And neither could they follow a word of our assimilated neutral English accents, which were equally a foreign tongue to them. With the best will in the world on both sides, there was an insurmountable block to cultural contact. Surmountable only by the levelling-down action of drink, by the universal language of the drunk.

I would not like it to be thought that while our menfolk were undergoing their self-inflicted test of endurance, Helen and I were patiently sitting on the front porch of our lodging house knitting socks, scarves and balaclavas for the needy soldiers. No fear: we were a flighty pair of emancipated fun-loving girls in those happy-go-lucky days, mad about dancing, men, flirting, beautiful clothes and all the vain fripperies that are the salt of the earth to females.

We were not averse to taking a drink or two but not always confined to the one place as our menfolk were prepared to be. That was far too deadly tedious for us. Our trouble was that we still enjoyed other things besides drinking, and we wanted to do them all, one after the other or all together. How we loved dressing up in all sorts of fantastic clothes and flirting around with the local clots. We would have liked a good old gossip with the local women too, but they only giggled at us uncomprehendingly.

Neither of us pretended to be bluestockings; we left that department strictly to our respective husbands and kept well out of it. We were both out-and-out lowbrows, to be exact, trading on a combination of our physical attributes—not meagre in quantity—and a self-confessed ignorance in literary matters. Helen was extremely skilled in various other practical ways, but when I was asked what I could do, apart from dancing, I was very hard put to find an answer. I was one of the rare exceptions in our literary circle who did not devour books.

The local clots were always a lot better looking than our highbrow husbands, who looked comically alike—both short and square in tweed jackets, check caps and corduroy trousers, with perhaps an additional stick or pipe. They were trying to pass themselves off as prosperous country squires, to fit in with the bucolic atmosphere. It was pretty much the same way they dressed in Chelsea or Soho in any case. Most probably the joint brain-power of the two of them would have weighed considerably more than that of the milling population of local clots at the fair scrambled together.

But it was not brains that Helen and I were after, it was scintillating life. And a brain is more of an impediment than not in the skirmishes of scintillating life. No brains at all was more accommodating to our purposes and left no hard feelings afterwards. We wanted simply to get outside the suffocation of the pub, to breathe fresh air, to move our bodies instead of our brains, to see the world going by, to leap up and down, to be released, for a breathing space, from drinking. Drinking which had become, instead of an enjoyment, a tyranny. We were two old-fashioned party girls who liked living it up, and our idea of living it up was not incarceration in a pub, day and night, with our highbrow husbands apparently happy as bog-boys to do so.

It must not be imagined, however, that when their lowbrow wives were absent, our brainy bog-boys were absorbed in discussing erudite matters. They very rarely touched literature, especially not in pubs, although in their sober lives literature was their greatest passion. They descended, in these pub-drinking bouts, to a pathetically infantile level, howling and shrieking their heads off at God-knows-what shared bawdiness. Ogling down the front of the barmaid's low-cut dress, poking surreptitious fingers down the cleft between her giant jiggling tits and boldly nipping at their fugitive tips, to fresh roars of laughter. That is what barmaids were for, was it not? In lewd words they were the ultimate in decadent Casanovas, and what they were going to do was nobody's business. Nor did they give a damn what we did when we left them. When the cats were away, the mice did play, with a vengeance. It was reciprocal: the cats were not backward either in going forward.

That is the awful thing about matrimony: anything is better than the bird in the hand. There is no solution but a change of birds, from a caged bird to a wild bird. Even if the change is from a bird of paradise to a blackbird. The stimulation is not in the relative quality of the birds, it is in the unknown quantity. And in this unknown quantity lies the magic. When that unknown quantity becomes known, the magic will disappear as quickly. The same goes for women again. There is no biological difference between their desires and those of men in this respect, any more than there is in the drinking respect. That deduction is more of men's wishful thinking again, more of men's flapdoodle. A wild unknown man, even if a far inferior man to the known tamed one, will inevitably be more exciting. The sterling integrity of the owned mate will serve but to rub in his stale tameness and his monotony. Therefore, the only differences between the sexes in this respect are conventional, circumstantial and economical.

Helen was one of the few women who was my genuine personal friend irrespective of Dylan; though she genuinely loved Dylan too. Most women made up to me (when they did) only because I was Dylan's appendage. One thing is sure and certain, that in the company of this mixed bag of pedigree and mongrel Celts, Helen from the unspeakable Midlands of England had more guts in her little English finger than any of us decadent Celts spawned together. She was a bombshell of glitter and glamour around whom the weak-kneed dependent Celts gravitated. We reached out towards her and clung to her like drowning men in high seas to a welcoming lighthouse. And that was the way she struck us too: as a blessed lighthouse in a storm.

Helen was one of the most generous women I ever met; I was the other one. But the aim of my generosity was not the enrichment of the receiver of my generosity, but the aggrandizement of the giver of it. I had learnt early at school that only by bringing chocolates with me and bribing the other children with them would they speak to me. My popularity, my tiny moment of glory was pitiably short-lived, as long as the chocolates lasted. And later on, in my drinking days, I was always trying desperately to recapture my tiny moment of glory, my popularity, by grand gestures of generosity. Absurd when I had not got two pennies to rub together. I left ridiculous tips to bedazzle waiters. I played at having money, at being rich. I had no sympathy for the poor little rich girl. There was no place I would have liked better to be than in her shining boots. I fished down-and-outs out of their gutters, when I was in the biggest gutter of all of them. I left the front door always open, as my fanatical father had told me to do, and asked the hypothetical stranger on the threshold to come inside in case he was—one never knows—the Christ Himself in person. By blindly following my fanatical father's optimistic dictums, our few precious possessions were continually being pinched from under our noses.

Helen's was a very different kind of generosity from mine; it was the genuine article. She did the things in private that really counted. She did the dirty work. She provided the practical essentials. She put us up whenever we needed to be put up. And, more important still, she put up with us, patiently, time and time again, however badly we behaved. She understood, she let it pass. There was nothing very glamorous about having us as guests. It was a thankless task. But she fed us just the same and it was food we needed, not drink! She provided the glamorous things for me too, and those I needed even more than food. I was starved for glamorous things, they were my food and drink. She ran me up beautiful dresses on her sewing machine, in a twinkling. All gay and flowery and flatteringly fitting in the right places, for a change. She bought me new comfortable-as-well-as-pretty shoes. I did not know that comfort and prettiness could exist together. I was able at last to throw away my old flapping-soled sandals that had crippled me for months on end. By dolling me up with all these pretty things, bought by herself, she was happy to make me prettier than herself. Not many friends would do that. Not any, except her. In Helen's place, I am pretty sure, I would not have been that generous. When she asked me to bring her back a piece of silk from abroad, I got it all right, but I could not hand it over to her on my return. It was already made up and draped across my starved-for-glamour back instead of hers. That was gratitude, that was.

The Celts have a strange belief that simply because they are Celts, they have the divine right to down all the drinks in sight (including the dregs) since, as everybody knows, it is not their fault; they can't help it because they are not like ordinary people. They think they have a divine compulsion to drink. This is their accepted cross. The host (or hostess) also had no choice but to accept the "Celtic Cross" or lose altogether their amusing talk and entertainment. A party was never a party without the Celts to drink up the dregs in all the glasses.

On this last holidaying visit to Puck Fair with Dylan, Helen and Bill MacAlpine, devilishly little of the elusive magic of Ireland did any of us see or feel or hear. We were all blind, unfeeling and deaf to its magic. The drink had ironed it all out of us as flat as a neutral country. We had drunk ourselves to a standstill, to a lie-still, to a grave-still. We were mummified; we were embalmed in alcohol. For all the magic that was in Ireland we might as well have been in Birmingham.

After this shameful orgy of bloating ourselves to near extinction, we were all down in the mouth and incapable of articulate speech. So we went back to our original occupations and tried very hard to regain our sanity.

I always found that when I turned to nature for my healing process whenever I was in mental distress, everything went better and fell into its proper place. Thus it was then in Laugharne, when I went back to my fumbling attempts at housekeeping and Dylan went back to his regular writing in his shed, with time off for gossiping with his buddies in the bow window of Brown's Hotel.

Coming back home to the all-too-familiar flatness of ordinary life was always the worst part after an excess of indulgence. It made one conclude one would have been better to have stayed where one was without craving new, more exciting things.

As I think I have said many times before, Heaven is not up there, in the pink clouds. It is in the secret greasy passages of the shell of the common snail with its two protuberant eyes on the very tip of two oily feelers. Just like in a poet I once knew.

Between my first visit and my last visit to Ireland lay the massacre of my first fine spirit of adventure. I had been transformed, in the civilizing pub interior, from a live and kicking animal into an inanimate root vegetable, unresponsive to anything outside alcohol. Responsive only to alcohol. Only alcohol could make the inanimate root vegetable alive and kicking again. But it was an artificially induced life that lasted only as long as the artificial inducement lasted. At the end I dropped deeper down than ever before. Then there was the pent-up waiting, buried down under the parched crust of the earth for the next liberating shower. Eventually the showers of liberation got shorter. The artificial life-giver had massacred my natural life. I was getting daily deader to the world than a dodo bird.

The driving impetus of my natural life was still kicking, but it was a different kind of kicking: it was no longer kicking for joy, it was the kicking of rage and frustration. A kicking against the bars of a wild animal trapped in a cage. And when it escaped in drink, God help anyone who got in its raging passage. There was no knowing what it might or might not do. It had no judgment at all. It was motivated by jungle instinct alone.

I never connected the growing pain in my side with drink—nor did anyone ever permit themselves to say one disapproving word against my drinking. It was the non-drinker who was disapproved of, looked down on, pitied. To add fuel to the lively prejudices against non-drinkers, Dylan and I had invented a verbal system of denigrating them. The dedicated, sober, serious, hard daily workers were denigrated by us as smug, self-satisfied, complacent prigs. We had collected a set of disparaging expressions for just such pompous, pathetically striving industrious beings, as we liked to picture them. Miserable nonentities, cowardly dolts, insignificant lily-livered sags and softies, on the same abysmal level as conscientious objectors, vegetarians and, the most crawling scum of all, of course: teetotallers.

I was extremely proud of my cast-iron stomach, which was capable of absorbing any amount of mixed alcoholic muck over indefinite periods of time and never once vomiting it up, as less noble stomachs were ignominiously forced to do. In this way, by retaining in my system all the destructive poisons of alcohol, I furthered their wrecking function. It would have been far better for me to have vomited up those poisons. But at that time I had never seen nor heard of the word "alcoholism" and I had no idea what it meant. Nor had Dylan. It was not so much escaping from reality that we were doing, because the drinking racket was our only practical reality. It was the only reality with which we were familiar. To us it was our normal living.

But even then, hooked as I must have been, well and good, on alcohol, I do remember, deep down, silently dreading the beginning—yet again—of those endless drinking binges. After the beginning, though, the dread disappeared and I went full steam ahead until I was lost to the world. But even then there was still a small stubborn block of resistance, a knot of opposition, a muffled cry of protest in me, that cried out in the dark, "This is not the way I would wish to be." And to that small desert island of detachment in me, from which I looked on and did not approve, I now owe my present precarious sobriety. I now owe my punishment of survival. For it is only in the punishment of survival that the full picture of the bitter consequences of my former drinking life are clearly revealed to me: the irreparable damage done to my battered brain, which wasn't much to start with but was even less by the end, and to my battered liver. I had always scoffed before at people who fussed so much about their livers, when my own was shot to bits. But I had not the good fortune to be snatched away, as Dylan was, in full drinking bloom; I was too stinking tough. Dylan always had all the good fortune.

12

From Stagnating in Florence
to Adventuring in Elba

In 1947, Margaret Taylor (wife of historian A.J.P. Taylor), our patroness, happened to get a windfall of three hundred pounds and most generously rented a posh villa in Italy to give us an exotic holiday for three months. It was called the Villa Beccaro at Scandicci, five miles from Florence. We brought our two children, Llewelyn and Aeron (about eight and four respectively) and also my sister Brigit with her small son, Tobias. We had never seen such luxury before: lovely grounds, terraces and even a swimming pool, which we used a lot. Dylan once accidentally fell in fully clothed!

After the long, tiring boat and train journey, Villa Beccaro seemed like paradise on earth. However, Dylan found that too much unaccustomed beauty soon palled. He disliked too much heat, for he could not work between noon and early evening. He got to loathe the "rasher-frying sun." In Italy I, however, came into my own, at last. It was a wine country and I loved wine; it was my favourite tipple. The people looked at me, instead of at Dylan. The men not only looked at me, they stripped me naked with their goggling eyes travelling round from breasts to bottom. I did not have a moment's peace when I was alone. To my acute embarrassment I dared not even stop to look in a shop window.

Dylan dutifully filled himself to the brim with wine, but I could tell that his heart wasn't in it. He made frequent visits to Florence, a journey that entailed taking a horse and cart to Scandicci, then a tram for nearly an hour. He sat for hours in the well-known Florentine café Giubbe Rosse, drinking wine and getting more and more depressed because there was nobody he could talk to in English. He wasn't used to wine; he was a beer drinker. His heart was yearning homewards, into dark bleak caverns below stairs where foaming-at-the-mouth brown liquid flowed freely and his cavernous voice bounced off the listening walls, and where no blinding spotlight of sun ever presumed to enter. He could not hold forth in Italy: nobody understood him! He was not going to waste his enjoyment time learning their language; he had enough trouble with his own. I never realized until now how much he must have suffered on that account; how terribly frustrated he must have felt without the communing word. Dylan without this was not Dylan: all his fascination hung on his humorous conversation. This fact was never more evident than when Italian poets came to call, for they were unable to converse together.

For me, it was very different. I loved going round Florence, gazing at everything new and exciting. Sucking up the foreign atmosphere, then joining him later at the café.

Nobody in Italy took a bit of notice of Dylan (only very few and far between "bluestockings" had even heard of him at that stage of his career). His reluctant role was now keeping the pouncer's hands off the desirable object. It must have been an entirely new sensation for him and not a pleasant one. I would be telling a big lie if I said that I did not gloat on this refreshing reversal of our roles. Oh, I did indeed, I gloated and gloated to my heart's content.

Dylan must have felt for the first time what it feels like to be the husband, the stooge of the desirable one, the hurdle stopping the gogglers from devouring the desirable one wholesale. It was just as I had felt for so long, for all our time together in England up till now. There I was the encumbering-him wife, the stone in the middle of his path. There is always too little or too much of a good thing, and in Italy there was a gross too many goggling eyes for me.

Dylan had no urge to travel, though he liked to fantasize about us travelling to exotic, faraway places, building sand-castles in the intoxicated air. But he was always better off where he was, with his old friends, old habits, old beverages, old climate and, above all, his own, or rather God's own, language. No man was less of an adventurer in foreign climes than Dylan, and no man or woman can change their inborn insular mentality. It was precisely that—his inborn insularity—that gave him the compact punch of his poems.

Dylan could adjust to any and every circumstance, but he always remained, both inside and outside, just the same: just Dylan. Had he lived twenty years in an igloo with the Eskimos, he would never have become an Eskimo in an igloo. He would always have been Dylan, perfectly at home, in an igloo. That was one of his great gifts: remaining always the same at heart.

In July, unable to bear the heat in Florence any longer, we all moved to the island of Elba, where we stayed, all packed together, in a small, very primitive hotel on the rocks by the sea. The proud manager of the hotel and his fat smiling wife (who did all the excellent cooking in the hotel) showed us the many improvements they had made during the winter. The *pièce de résistance* was a shining white, dazzling bathroom, with a spotless bath and all the modern innovations. I was amazed and delighted to see such an unlikely thing in such a small

hotel! When I complimented the friendly couple on it and
asked them if I could have a bath in it later, they began to look
exceedingly shifty and explained to me, in acute embarrassment, that the water had not yet been laid on. They expected
it any day now. The water, to our great disappointment, never
was laid on while we were there: for ten dry days. The bathroom had everything essential for body-cleanliness, bar the
water.

Elba was not at all fashionable then and very cheap. It was
much more our style, even though we had to trail down
parched paths under that peeling-us-in-strips-of-red-skin sun
to the sea, which was a scorching bath of stinging ink. Only
in the boiling seas of Elba did I ever see Dylan lying in a rock-
pool in a few inches of water—reading the *New Statesman*
with his hat on and an old stub of a cigarette drooping out the
side of his mouth. Like a snail or an Englishman, he carried
his home with him wherever he went. Far from assimilating
into the new country he went to, he expected the new country to conform to him. Surprisingly, after a very short time in
Dylan's company, the people on Elba were invariably
charmed to conform to him, even with no communal language, which says something for his winning charms.

For a habitually drinking person, travelling from place to
place really means travelling from bar to bar. The only mean-
ingful things that change are the various types of bars, the
various types of drinks in the bars, the various types of
drinkers in the bars and the various types of languages spoken
in the bars. Devil-a-bit this narrow traveller sees or cares
about what goes on outside the bars. He is interested only in
that self-same monotonous row of fluctuating bottles that
hold him in thrall, a mummified witness to their ascendancy
over him. And when we got to the sea somehow, in that wine-
making island in August, the sea was made of purple ink.

13
The Advance of the Cavalry
of Seahorses

When we moved, in 1949, to the Boat House in Laugharne (bought for us by Margaret Taylor), there was the thrill of the incoming and outgoing tides surging in and slowly subsiding out. They invaded our backyard regularly and unpredictably. They rushed in at tumultuous speed as high as the stone wall that surrounded the grassy harbour and were a constant peril for the children of unthinking parents and, incidentally, also for the unthinking parents themselves, of whom I was one. We never bothered to get the timing of the tides worked out properly, of their later-every-day entries and exits. It was not from not caring, but from pure fecklessness and my idiotic conviction of our impregnability, which amounts to roughly the same thing. They very nearly did sweep us away back out to sea; it was a near thing, and we passed some very nasty moments of not knowing what was going to happen to us in our touch-and-go predicaments. But were we warned off from bathing in the stream of the estuary with no knowledge of when the tides would come in? Not a bit of it. The risk added spice to our bathing excitement. So we went on blithely tempting fate and getting away with it. We certainly did not deserve to. I got to feel that I was invincible, a very unwise way to feel. Those treacherous tides swept away other local children quite regularly, and their parents reacted with an apparent resignation as to an Act of God. The tides could equally easily have swept away mine while they were playing thoughtlessly on the rocks nearby or later tossing to and fro in their little rowboat, the *Cuckoo*. Whoever took care of my children, I would like to thank them now, deeply and earnestly from the bottom of my remorseful soul. I am fully aware I did not mind their safety adequately. I can only say, in my defence, that I was nearly always present with them.

I was, in fact, leading them on. I had invented this new drink which, to my moron's mind, beautifully combined virtue and courage. It was a large glass of pure milk, personifying virtue, very generously laced with pure whisky, personifying courage. On this emboldening combination of nourishing ingredients, I was prepared to vault on the backs of a battalion of white horses charging in on the tide. To grip them by their tossing manes and, flat on my stomach, to ride them into harbour. I flung myself recklessly off the backyard wall into the turmoil of boiling-up seas below. It was a marvellous feeling: my cunning concoction had obliterated fear. I was the great nature dominator. I was the great bareback rider on the heaving rump of the sea! That is the way I saw it then in my euphoria through whisky eyes. The milk, such as it was, churning quietly below stairs, played a very minor role in my act of bravura.

After the daily tides had raged into our backyard, up the steps and as far as the kitchen door and into the kitchen on high spring tides, the still-shuddering waters settled down briefly before they imperceptibly turned tail and very gradually seeped back out to sea again. It was in this benign pause that I had to strip off my outer clothes and, in only my underwear, swim out to collect the almost submerged nappies I had forgotten, still damply flapping about on the line. But this was no hardship for me: it was all part of the fun and joking with the children, and we all enjoyed the screaming lark. The difficulty was to calm them down and make them come in quietly for their supper, which most probably was that inescapably dull-as-ditchwater semolina pudding again. I had a permanent guilt that I was unable to make anything more interesting for them: a guilt, however, that never made me learn something more interesting.

This wild larking life, often with gangs of the Laugharne children joining in, was good for my children for as long as it lasted and for as long as they managed to keep their heads above the vacillating waters of our capricious estuary.

Dylan was exempt from these external dangers. He preferred to drown himself internally, and not with cold water. Cold water did not agree with him internally or externally. He was as allergic to cold water on his body as a horrified hissing cat; and he never once risked joining us in our much-too-cold and, for him, unpleasantly muddy estuary. He did not revel in the mud as the children and I did. He very sensibly knew what he liked, and what he liked was sufficient for him.

Unlike me, he was content to let nature dominate him. If it rained, Dylan went inside. Whereas, if it rained, I went outside. Dylan had no wish, as I had, to explore new uncharted avenues. His new uncharted avenues were all dormant in his head already, in words, and he preferred to explore them by his fireside. He preferred sitting with a heaped-up plate of all his favourite spicy goodies on his knees and a bottle of some soft fizzy drink to swill them down, listening gleefully to the cricket scores on the radio. A male indulgence permitted only when I was not present.

But I must admit that cold water, taken internally, did not agree with me either, and I can't remember a single occasion on which either of us actually drank water, hot or cold. It was much too flat to bear contemplating. And though I have often tried since to imagine myself in the desert, dying for want of water, I seem unable to build up a genuine craving for it. It still represents to me the ultimate reduction of the proud personality, when of course it is, as I ought to have learned by now, the proud personality who flourishes on water. But the anti-water conditioning built in me from my alcoholic environment is still too strong, is still a stone wall of resistance, not to be shifted so fast or so easily by the feeble evocation of water from a dripping tap in the kitchen sink. More ruthless time must pass, more relentless reconditioning, before I can see the sparkling fascination, feel the thirst-quenching ecstasies of water in the desert—let alone before I can slaver at the tap in the kitchen sink. I will be lucky if I can achieve that sublime ignominy this side of the grave.

Dylan was intrinsically much more sensible than I was (notwithstanding his high-flying language in writing). He knew who he was, what he wanted, and he went straight for it and he got it. It may not have looked as though Dylan knew where he was going, but he had it all worked out somewhere in the recesses of his head, right up until death. Although it proved inordinately tough to polish off that "frail" constitution of his in romantic time, he continued to hammer at it with blows of asphyxiating neat spirits, and they slowly and reluctantly did the job. He had told his body to stop before he was forty years old, but his body was unwilling to stop and he only *just* made it. To what length of unnecessary pain can a body be pushed? Such a little body Dylan had, to treat it so.

I find it very hard now to reconcile my overscrupulous perfectionism in minute details of the cleanliness, dressing and feeding of my small children, with my reckless disregard of overwhelming physical dangers, like the tides and the bombs. But no doubt I shall be told by those of my own kind that it is a typical alcoholic trait, and as such, a part of my disease.

The harder I drank, the more furiously I flung myself into oblivion in the night, as though I was never going to wake up again, and the more furiously I exercised my broken body the next morning, forcing it into agonizing movement. I put precisely the same amount of passion into breaking up my body at night, as I did into painstakingly reconstructing it in the morning. It was a senseless repetition of two directly conflicting instincts.

Nothing will convince an alcoholic that he has not sinned; his sense of sinning is so strong in him, so overwhelming. And he is dead right too, because he has committed the worst sin he can commit: he has sinned against the original sacred flame of life in himself, and knows it. It is no good telling him that it is not his fault, that he is powerless over alcohol, because he knows better. But what remains in himself of his original sacred flame of life? If it is still strong enough in him and if he wants badly enough to be cured, it will cure him. If it is not, his flame will flicker out and he will be overwhelmed by sinning alcohol. Others can help him, but they cannot cure him; his original sacred flame of life alone can cure him.

14

The Art of Treading on Flatfish

The story of one of my passionate occupations in the estuary at Laugharne is an apt example of the furiously antagonistic relationship I had with my daughter on the surface, while underneath I simply adored her and spoilt her to death.

The art of treading on flatfish in the estuary with the tide out enticed me. It is an entirely different and more joyful proposition than the art of trout-tickling. But it is an art all the same and one that can, at times, miraculously succeed. It is done, for a start, over a great expanse of mud and sand (more mud than sand), in a thin shallow stream between muddy banks of half-fresh, half-salt water left after the tide has gone out. Over this great expanse is another even greater expanse of misty sky with water birds swirling and swishing, croaking across it. You are sandwiched between black sinking mud underfoot and delirious dream-sky overhead.

You must go to this job barefoot with trousers rolled up high, for in places on the way, you sink into the mud up to the knees. But the ground under the stream in the middle of this wilderness of mud and sky sinks in hardly at all, probably because it is mixed with more sand than mud and remains fixed there by the presence of the water. It is this more solid surface that allows you to hold down a flatfish with your bare foot. Otherwise it would simply sink down further and disappear under the mud.

Standing quietly on comparatively hard ground in the water of the stream, you must proceed to shuffle along with all your sensibilities concentrated in the soles of your feet. The instant that you feel beneath the sole of one foot a slightly rising, faintly vibrating mound that instantly buries itself deeper into the ground, you must stay dead still as though you had been planted there, tree-like, for all eternity. You must not leap in the air with a yell as your first instinct tempts you to do.

After a plausible period of waiting in this rather grotesque position in order to establish stagnant harmony with nature and to calm down your own nerves and those of the flatfish, you must bend down and carefully place your hands around the circumference of the flatfish without removing your foot from it. Then, when you have a good grip, you simply lift up your foot and nonchalantly toss your now slumberous catch well over the sludgy bank opposite.

Flatfish have been known, once carelessly tossed over the bank, to lurch back over the mud and to wallow back into their stream before you can look around, which is most irritating, to put it mildly. But when you successfully get the fish on dry land, what an inexpressible sense of triumph that is! What an incomparable sense of delight! Nothing can compare with it for sheer untrammelled exultation of divine life in nature. Not quite so divine for the fish perhaps, but then give and take is the law of nature, is it not?

However, my untrammelled exultation of divine life in nature was abruptly marred by my small daughter, who had followed along on the opposite bank, regularly stooping and, one by one, throwing back into the water the hard-earned flatfish that I had laid out so carefully on the bank for my collection later on. I could not believe my eyes. I could have killed her! I was speechless with rage. How could she dare to spoil all my joy without a qualm of conscience? *She* could and did; she was enjoying doing the mincing little miss reproving her brutal mother for her cruelty to dumb animals. I tried indignantly to remonstrate with her but to no avail. I was mad but impotent. The damage was done. I was standing there blocked in the water below her and she was presiding over me on the bank, like an irate schoolteacher ticking me off. We were getting nowhere; we were struck at cross purposes with daggers drawn. Suddenly she made a *volte-face* and resorted to tears. She made out she was crying because she was sorry for the poor little fish. Poor little fish, my eyeballs! I was not going to fall for *that* one. She was hurting poor little me far more than I was hurting the poor little fish!

It was an enigma, all the same, how my small daughter got those crocodile tears to ooze out so pityingly for the fish; so pitifully for herself. But she was not my daughter for nothing. I knew her play-acting only too well; it was all too familiar to me, I had only to look inwards. I had play-acted all my life, and it was only in these rare precious moments alone, when I was face to face with the vast impersonality of life and death in nature, that I was not play-acting. There was no need to, no need to take anybody in: there was nobody there to be taken in. Not until my daughter came along anyhow. Then we were competing against each other, doing our utmost to outdo each other in furious antagonism.

Oh yes, it was an act all right, even if she did not know that it was an act at that young time. She fancied herself in the part of the rescuer of the downtrodden. How often had I too, in the past, fancied myself in the part of the rescuer of the downtrodden. Only my downtrodden were mostly talking animals.

"A fish can't feel, you fool," I shouted at her. "It is not a dumb animal. It is a cold-blooded Pisces like you."

But of course that was not true, as I discovered later on when I chucked a live flatfish into a frying pan of scalding oil and it promptly leapt out onto the floor. A flatfish *can* feel; I could see that, or was it only, as I had been told, an automatic reflex that happened to animals immediately after the death blow? I picked the fish up off the floor with a rag and chucked it back into its scalding frying pan to put it out of its distressful dilemma. But it would not stop its spasmodic jerks. It went on and on and refused to stop and nearly jerked out of the frying pan again. It was getting beyond a joke. My patience, never very lengthy, had given out. At long last the flatfish consented to settle down, albeit with its back still stiffly arched.

It was scalding hot and half raw as I tore into it in my impatience but, I have got to say, I never tasted anything so delicious in my whole lifetime. Such is the potency of devouring one's very own victim, captured with the sole of one's very own foot.

15

For Sheer Lovableness

For sheer lovableness there was nobody to beat Dylan. But lovableness was no aid to the rigidity that is necessary for an artist, and which Dylan lacked. No aid to the ruthlessness necessary to the artist, which Dylan also lacked. He was incapable of barring the door against his devoted friends, to whom he also was devoted, and facing up to stark austerity for the sake of his body and his work. His devoted friends always came first. He never said no to them: he did not know how to say no to them. He was always willing to oblige and, by obliging them, oblige himself too.

Dylan's sheer lovableness was, to my mind, his chief trouble: he had no defence against being eaten alive by sycophants and harpies. My chief trouble was, I can only conclude, that I selfishly wanted all his sheer lovableness for myself alone.

I could not believe at first that Dylan actually went to bed with other women. I refused to believe it: my porcupine quills rose in revolt. Probably everybody in every bar all over

London knew about it, but not I, tucked away with our offspring in my isolation. Dylan's devoted friends patted themselves on the back for their tactful muteness, their admirable
loyalty to Dylan. In the end, however, I had no choice but to
believe in Dylan's treachery.

Dylan betrayed me habitually almost from the very beginning of our love idyll. At the start he was much more discreet,
and he never betrayed me in our country place in front of the
neighbours, with the result that they considered him a long-
suffering saint in comparison to me. Only in far-distant invisible places did he revel in his randiness. My doubts started
after weeks of silent absences. Dylan's passionate words of
love to me, I am convinced even now, were dead true while he
was declaiming them. He was a born actor, and it is perfectly
possible to truly love one important person, while at the same
time fooling around with another unimportant person. Although, with drink, I managed to blot out nearly all the
loving closeness of our volatile love. I could never be sure if I
really loved Dylan or not. Or if Dylan really loved me or
not—and not just in declaimed and written words.

To Dylan I was beyond criticism. I don't remember him
ever criticising anything about me; what I did was always okay
by him. Except once, when he discovered by chance I had
spent a wicked night with a voluptuous blond pianist in
Cardiff, he threw a blunt knife at me which missed its mark
by yards. And as the final ironic touch to my misdemeanour,
the pianist, so sensual on the keys, was impotent in bed. I was
nonplussed; such a failure of the male member to rise to the
occasion had never occurred to me before. I had expected, as
on former occasions, my mere proximity to cause the male
member to spring to attention. It was highly embarrassing,
although "highly" is a hardly appropriate word in this context.
But even in drink, as I undoubtedly was (who is brave enough
to contemplate copulation without being well primed up
first?), I was much too shy and inhibited to mention to him

his shortcomings in the amorous proceedings. And I did not dream of touching the limp thing. I was much too well brought up. So was he, apparently. He did not mention it either, or even apologise for his inadequacy. We both pretended everything was as it ought to be, that we noticed nothing unusual, out of place or missing. We both just lay there, as though struck with paralysis. I was wearing my Isadora Duncan tunic, gazing miserably up at the ceiling and waiting for my blond god to impatiently strip my negligee from my concealed body, for something to happen, until eventually we both dropped off into a fitful, not very friendly sleep. Schubert never sounded quite the same to me afterwards.

This little, rather pathetic attempt of mine at getting my own back on Dylan, at having my own independent Arabian night, fell on a very flat note indeed. It was the first and last time I attempted a calculated love affair. It had been a deliberate deception, and deliberate deceptions never worked for me. I was not clever enough to brazen them out.

I have not yet mentioned the preliminaries, to what painstaking lengths I was prepared to go to prepare for my wicked night in a posh hotel in Cardiff. The truth of the matter was that I was terrified by what I was about to do, but that very fact was a challenge to me. I would have been a coward, in my own estimation, had I slyly sneaked out of it. Therefore, in order to present myself suitably attired at the meeting place in the hotel lounge, I had to buy some new clothes, and for that I needed money, which obviously I had not got. The only way I could think of to get any money was to go back down to our bogs (I had wisely brought the key with me), while pretending to Dylan that I was staying with his parents, and to sell for next to nothing nearly every one of the hard-earned earthly possessions, almost every little twig that had gone into the weaving of our love-nest. It did not take long; I practically gave everything away. So thus, with this considerable sum of money, I went on to Cardiff to deck myself out, good and proper, for my seduction act.

That lust for buying, so long repressed, that delirious buying without stint, was the only fun part of my misadventure. I felt terrific in my bandbox finery. I had never before in my life had so many luxurious garments at one time. It went to my head much more than a mouldy drink could ever have done. All would have been perfect had I not been weighed down by the thought of the coming meeting, which hung over me like a hangman's noose.

Unfortunately I had not calculated on the keen powers of observation of Dylan's mother, an unpardonable slip of mine. She reported immediately to Dylan the exact number of nights I had slept under his parents' roof. There was one stray night left unaccounted for, which even Dylan, with his gift for blinding himself to what he did not wish to see, could not ignore completely. Hence the half-hearted knife flung vaguely in my direction. Had Dylan been a Sicilian I would not be here to tell the tale. Trust his mother to smell out the rat in my carelessly laid plan. It was my one and only *calculated* infidelity to Dylan, and what a farce it turned out to be. A criminal should never underestimate the accidental slip, even in a seemingly foolproof plan. I had banked on Dylan's drinking obtuseness, but overlooked his mother's sober astuteness.

This particular mortification, this farcical disaster of mine, this defrocking of Schubert from his throne left a nastier taste than usual in the mouth. The blotting paper of alcohol has not blotted it out to this day in my shaky sobriety.

There is no end to infidelity and there is no possibility of fidelity existing, because even one who practises fidelity to the letter cannot stop the infidelity of his thoughts. He cannot stop his longing for the unknowable. Even in Dylan's and my marriage of twin souls, which could not have been more unchained, uncaged, unbridled, there was still the slot of convention to be escaped from. In spite of our refusal to accept the conventions, we had married each other, we did the "done" thing. I really can't think why we got married; we had been living together in sin, in perfect artist fashion, for a year or more previously. So why did we get married? It changed nothing. We went on exactly as before. It was an act of inspired madness. It was certainly not for economic gain, for we were both penniless and proud of it. We were still young enough then to take pride in penury, although we got over that. Nor was it to make the birth of our first child respectable, to give him the honourable name of Thomas. We would never have allowed so contemptible a bourgeois concept to enter our lofty heads. We heartily despised such humbling qualities as prudence, providence, looking to the future, providing for old age, even to the triangle of earth to be buried in, and all those far-fetched horrible things that could never possibly happen to us. And avarice, meanness, stinginess were the worst of all crimes for us. They were a threat to our bread and butter—or rather to what swilled the bread and butter down. We ourselves were never mean. We bought drinks liberally round the house, on tick. And put off the paying headache for the morrow, for the morrow of the patroness. It is easy not to be mean when there is nothing in the kitty to be mean with. The more that is in the kitty, the more difficult it is, apparently, not to be mean.

Could the reason for our marriage possibly have been one so banal as that we loved each other, so got married as a conditioned reflex to loving each other? As unthinkingly as Pavlov's dogs at the ringing of bells. There was no limit to our unthinkingness, it is true. At that time, the sun revolved around our love, not our love around the sun. We were blinded by it like moles emerging from the long dark tunnels of the earth. Drunken moles at that.

There were days when I did undoubtedly love Dylan! We were like the titmouse family: nestling deep down together in our soft mounds of feathers with never a cross word passing either of our lips. On other days I could cheerfully have slaughtered Dylan for his acts of infidelity in the big wicked city of London, when away from me and our lullabying home.

Among Dylan's many attractive qualities was his famous unforgettable voice. He was known to some of his oldest friends simply as The Voice. It was surely the only time in history, though I may be wrong, that a poet has been blessed with a voice of the same calibre as his poems. A voice to match the music, the volume, the richness, the unhurried timing of his words. His throbbing voice carried him beyond the restrictions of his physical stature and took his words beyond the frontiers of his world, extending, more and more sonorously, into the infinity of foreign languages.

The combination of his potent voice, his superabundance of charm and, above all, his genius gift for constructing poems doomed Dylan right from his prodigious beginnings. Creatively his gifts were a curse and not a blessing. Had he not had all the extra social attributes, the ephemeral frills, he might still have been plugging away at his tortuous poems, making them clearer and clearer all the time. There was a surfeit of humanity in Dylan that interfered with his austerity as a poet. This was his undoing. Distance for a poet or any artist is all-important. Every artist needs both distance and company at the right times and in the right proportions, hard as that is to achieve.

Dylan loved people; he was made to have people around him, any people. He was utterly without that protective social antagonism with which most people preserve their precious private lives. Words were wonderful to him in a separate sealed department, but they had to wait for the pleasure of his people.

Poetry is not only a brainy thing. It is an incalculable combination of incalculables. It is a spontaneous capacity to catch—on the wing, out of a packed universe—the one crucial elusive thing that the poet needs to make his line rise and fly. To raise it from flatness into flight. To make it sing. To make it into poetry. One is or is not a poet. And a poem is a lucky happening out of that split second of understanding between poet and universe.

Reading his own work was always an exhausting emotional exercise for Dylan. Yet he did not hesitate to put the same fervour, if not more, into poetry inferior to his own, right after reading a batch of his own poems. Instead of being a good showman and building up to a high spot with his own poems, he preferred to get them out of the way first.

Dylan preferred reading other poets' poems, so he read his own first to get the dirty work out of the way. His own poems were the dirty work! Other poets' poems were fun work. This was not false modesty on his part; it was, on the contrary, complete arrogance, complete acceptance of the supremacy of his work. He could afford to be blithely indifferent to the temporary impression it made, because he was so certain of its permanent impression. Also, when reading other people's poems he was on firm ground, whereas, when reading his own, he was on distinctly marshy ground. More than that, it made him truly happy to make a bad poem sound like a beautiful one. Or, if it was too sorely tempting, to make a rollicking parody out of it! Or to get the nerve-vibrating throbbing best out of one of his favourite great ones. He inevitably accepted, as a matter of course, that he in particular should have been the chosen one to recite the precious material. This is the customary reaction of all those who are born great. They have no need for, no use for and no time for conceit, which, in one sense I suppose, is a greater form of conceit. Just as some men use their skilful hands as tools to work with, so Dylan used his skilful head as a tool. And he took it, his handy-head, as the handy-men take their hands, for granted.

Though Dylan was packed with brains, he looked the opposite, he behaved the opposite and he spoke the opposite of the popular conception of a bespectacled scholarly intellectual, absorbed in his bone-dry studies, to the exclusion of

the superficialities of lesser men. Dylan had no bone-dry
studies and he loved the superficialities of lesser men. He
was so fastiduous not to parade his brains in public that
there was no telling that he possessed such a profound mind
as was revealed in his writing. He did not use his brain-power
on brainy subjects, on improving his brain for instance. He
evidently felt that there was no room for improvement. So he
steadfastly wasted his brains on pure and simple drinking
enjoyment, which represented to him a relaxing foam-bath in
delicious contrast to his private battleground of words.

Only when doing his own work did all his concentrated
hidden intellectual powers come simultaneously into action.
He did not like talking about his own work, and very rarely
did so unless pushed into a poet's corner from which there
was no hope of escaping. He liked much better to pass himself off as merely a clever verbal quipper, a deft twister of
words or a teller of rambling whimsical tales, the point of
which lay in their pointlessness and interminability. He liked,
best of all, to act the clown. With his malleable appearance,
broken tooth and all, no great transformation was necessary.
And he laughed as loudly at himself as anybody.

Like Oscar Wilde in his prison, Dylan could make a cold
cell sparkle with warmth. He could make miserable devils
who had not smiled in months, who had not laughed in years,
crackle open—surprising themselves—with crackling laughter. More than Wilde's or Dylan's wit, it was the touch of their
old reciprocal humanity that did the trick. Both Wilde and
Dylan were the rare possessors of the authentic joy of life in
all its tiniest tributaries. And this mutual joy of life they managed to spread wherever they went.

Even when Dylan was sober and sick first thing in the
morning, after coughing up quantities of yellow slimy bile
into a bucket, he was only briefly laid out and amazingly
mute. He good-naturedly accepted his sickness as the natural
plight of every man worthy to be called a man. And once the

worst was over, he tended to revel in his sickness, to luxuriate in the extra attentions of his sickbed and to moan feebly for his mother's panacea for all ills: hot milk with bread broken up and a good dollop of salt in it. The salt was evidently essential to his cure and sure enough, in no time at all, he was on his feet again, making pubwards. I swear that he was happier sipping his comforting mother's mixture than dutifully downing his legend of beer. But, of course, these men are not allowed such baby slops except when sick.

Dylan was a professional baby. He would never grow up. He had made up his mind not to. He always wore his baby boy's fancy pants of whimsicality. He knew exactly what he was doing. It was a lot easier to get by that way, without too much hard labour, and it went down like hot-cakes with both young and old alike. He could get away with all sorts of naughty sayings and doings, all sorts of wicked outrageous mischief that nobody else, because they were grown up, could ever possibly be permitted to perpetrate. He could boldly ask, from out of the sweet innocence of his dear little soul, for extravagant favours, usually granted, that no grown-up would have the nerve to propose. Only because he was precisely what he intended to be, everybody's lovable professional baby.

It is an accepted fact now that immaturity is one of the scapeways of an alcoholic. His desire for a drink comes before intelligence, and can turn off the tap of intelligence. It might even be quite possible to suppose that the bigger the brain, the bigger the desire to submerge it in drink. It must be a dreadful weight to carry around all the long day and all the long night, to have to listen to its unsubmergible ticking.

Instead of howling with protest at his public suicide, everybody laughed and praised Dylan for his tragicomic performance. Dylan had an ancient, out-of-the-cave conception that his drinking prowess made him appear even more manly, more of a swashbuckling he-man, more of a superman among his fellow men. His genius, he felt, was a black mark against

him in these sporting trials of his muscled manliness of resistance. However fiercely he drew back his forearm against his
upper arm to illustrate his bulging biceps, there was not a rip-
ple of muscle to be detected in the snowy, soft smoothness.
Not even under a magnifying glass. Nobody expected an
abnormal genius to be a strong-arm man, anything but a common ordinary man. But Dylan had to prove at all costs that he
was a man like any other, more than any other, brushing aside
his unique gift of genius as so much dust and ashes. And his
way of proving it was by drinking more and faster than any
other man. He did not stop to think that he was proving his
point to a bunch of fools as stoned and as foolish as he was.
He did not stop to think—it is as simple as that. Drinking
people do not stop to think, and that's that.

Dylan was spared the tormenting problem of most young
men setting out in life of having to decide what to do or what
not to do to earn their livings and justify their existence. When
he had time off from drinking company, there was nothing in
the world Dylan could do but write. But it is a calumny to suggest, as some people did, that he was sometimes drunk when
he was writing. He may have experimented once out of curiosity to see the results of drunken writing but, once seen, he
never repeated the experiment. Normally he was never drunk
when writing. God forbid! It would have been a blasphemy to
Dylan—as to all self-respecting writers.

Dylan's sober writing was already drunk with words and
his natural fantasies already far too high-flown for comfortable consumption. He knew only too well that drunken writing when reread in sobriety was revealed as junk. And he
knew also, only too painfully, that there was no easy way, no
painless way, to produce good writing. Dylan knew only the
hard way—of laboured construction of weighted word upon
weighted word—to achieve his lighted-up heavens in the air.
He used a system identical to a builder calculating the placing
of the stones in a wall he is constructing. The only difference

between them that I can see was that Dylan took a lot longer to place his words. The builder, even taking his time, finished sooner and got more money for his work.

Dylan was totally lacking in competitive spirit, in that urge to beat his rival at all costs, to get to the top. As far as he was concerned, his top place was already assured. But although Dylan had no spirit of competition where his writing abilities were concerned, where his drinking prowess was concerned he had as rampant a spirit of competition as any of the bubbly-jock boys. For the noble cause of proving his superiority over all shapes and sizes of comers, he was prepared to pour down pint after pint of draught-bitter beer. He was prepared to blow up his once small flat belly to the bursting point. No writhing agonies of distortion of his frail flesh, no overflowing, vile eruptions of churning regurgitated beer were too great a sacrifice for winning the drinking stakes. The winner was the one who got down the most beer in the least time, while still remaining tottering on his pins. And Dylan would sooner have burst than lose his leadership of the "boys." He could let down a woman with the greatest of ease, they were two a penny, but he could not let down the "boys," for then he would be letting down the supreme honour of the drinking fellowship. And that, of course, was unthinkable.

All for show, it was done, all for show. An apparently sane man was prepared to kill himself, all for show. An apparently sane man who was a genius was prepared to be so unbelievably stupid as to subject himself, of his own free will, to so criminal a waste of his genius, all for show. An apparently sane man who was exceptionally bright and intelligent in everything except the drinking thing was prepared to go through this primitive, painful, puerile test of his drinking capacity and endurance, all for show. It is an unbelievably frivolous fact. And he was not the only one; there are many more apparently sane men, exceptionally bright and intelligent in everything except the drinking thing, who are prepared to do this same stupid thing, all for show.

When there wasn't enough time for Dylan to write, he lamented loudly. When there was too much time to write, with not enough distractions, Dylan became gloomily oppressed at the size of the staring-him-in-the-face vacuum to be meticulously, never-endingly filled up. Like an ant walking across a gigantic blank page. So he gave it up as a hopeless job and staged the usual unoriginal escape. Too much time is as bad as too little time—it is a very delicate balance.

Some days when Dylan was in his work hut and felt too languid to start hammering at his recalcitrant words, he relapsed into reading one of the detective books out of the store of them that he always kept hidden there. They were pleasantly soporific—even if afterwards he felt guiltily wicked about it. I could always tell, as I was walking past his work hut on my afternoon walks with our children, when Dylan was playing truant from his writing: there was no reassuring sound of his usual muttering and mumbling incantations from inside.

Dylan was also by lazy nature one of the least envious of people. Except for posh people's money. But that was a malady that no amount of money could ever assuage. We both of us needed money desperately, adored spending it on all the wrong things and never had enough of it. We were hopeless spendthrifts. In his heart of hearts he was convinced that for the poet poverty was an imperative. He was adept at courting poverty, never leaving a cent unspent; joyously as he loved money, riotously as he spent it till it was all spent (and this goes for me too), it was an unwritten law that poverty was for the poet. Poverty and, preferably for the perfectionist, an early agonizing death thrown in too. Dylan scrupulously fulfilled both these romantic conditions.

When he had taken more than enough alcohol, though he was fit to burst, he went on forcing it down just for show. Or at the beginning just for show, but later on, just for not being able to do without it. For a man who badly needs to drink does not give a fuck if drink makes a fool of him or not. There are always plenty of other fools as plastered as himself and as scintillating as himself, with no ears but their own enchanted ears to hear them. For a man who wants drink, nothing will stop him: neither low lucre nor perforated liver.

Lack of the necessary "filthy lucre" was never an insuperable problem for Dylan. It was only the price of the first preliminary drink that was the sticky bit. It was the golden key that opened the tap to all the following ones. After which, all was plain drinking. And if one area proved unproductive, an "experienced sponger" made a rapid geographical change for a more productive area. So Dylan sponged shamelessly. He had a superabundance of entertainment value. There was never any danger of his dying of thirst. It was a typical trader's bargain. The well-heeled wanted entertainment, so they paid for it, and got it—more even than they bargained for. Dylan, as usual, was the eventual loser, since he gave more than he got. He was not capable of giving halves—so he gave his whole self, wholeheartedly. But neither was he capable of taking drink in halves. Neither of us believed in half measures.

It was a real pity for us that we both had such generous souls at the expense of others and at the expense of our future mutilated bodies. We used to think, Dylan and I, that everybody who drank with us was like us: they drank till they dropped. But obviously they could not have been as thoughtlessly idiotic as we were. Many of the people who drank with us did it carefully, in cautious moderation, but it was not so evident to us, in our way-ahead-of-them excesses. Only Dylan's city clan were dedicated drinkers like us. Their loyalty to us and to our regular bars was absolute. They stuck to us like limpets to the bitter end: from 10:30 a.m. till 10:30 p.m. with an afternoon drinking club in between—in twelve-hour sessions. They can't all have been gentlemen of private means—far from it. They mostly looked as scruffily shabby as us and as nearly always broke. It was one of the sacred laws of our drinking jungle that whoever was in the money was honour bound to shell it out among his chosen buddies. Too bad for the chosen buddy who was most frequently in the money. But the professional penniless bums were not allowed an exemption from the drinker's imperative. As soon as it became blatantly obvious that they were there only for what they could get and had no intention whatsoever of offering any back, then the treacherous offender was instantly shoved out into ignominious schoolboy "coventry." Once banished, never to return.

In those squalid London pubs that Dylan and I loved to frequent (the squalider the better to our pseudo-romantic way of thinking), the emphasis was on the quantity rather than the quality of the alcohol. It was also on the quantity of nonstop gabble rather than on the quality of leisurely conversation. Pubs are one of the great levellers of the public values of important people. Death is another. Inside pubs all the people, or nearly all of them, become one big temporarily united family under the influence of alcohol. As soon as they get outside the pubs, of course, some people reassume their previous public values in a shamefaced hurry, brushing aside the unimportant pick-ups of the evening without so much as bidding them good night.

In London we would go from the pub straight to an afternoon drinking club. These iniquitous dives, of which somebody in the company had to be a member, opened only in the afternoons. Their sole attraction was that they filled in the vacuum of time between the pubs' closing in the afternoon and opening in the evening. But after a very short time in these sordid clubs it became evident that not only were the miserable drinks watered down, but they cost double the price of lawful drinks. These hiding holes in the mean streets had all the tedium of station waiting rooms: waiting, in this case, for the boisterous noise of the pub to come roaring into our straining-for-it ears. In this wasteful and disgraceful manner, whole precious days were totally obliterated. Only at the final closing time of the pubs, when we were dead to the world, were we usually just about able to stagger back to pass out on some unknown squalid couch. But we were naïvely young then, and tomorrow was another day. With tomorrow came reinforcements to start all over again the identical killing routine. Until, thanks to the drunkard's Lord, the money ran dry and we had no choice but to pack up our meagre belongings and go back to our dull but healthier country vegetation.

Dylan was not a visibly depressed kind of person. He had neither the inclination nor the time. The spiritual depression of accumulated alcohol never quite caught up with him. Not till America crashed down on him with its pile of cement skyscrapers and buried him alive. Then he was a visibly depressed kind of person—but never silenced. Dylan was normally an incredibly jolly person—with no material reason in the world to be jolly. With every material reason in the world against his being jolly. His unsuppressible jolliness came from inside him, not from outside circumstances, so there was nothing he could do about it. Of course he had his glooms, mostly lack-of-money glooms. But they were comparatively lightweight and short-lived. Dylan loved the world and all the people in it. That was his trouble. It was as hard for him to turn his back on the world and all the people in it as it is for a pretty girl to get old.

Alcohol, though a most important prop to Dylan, was not the be-all and end-all of life to him. As much as the drink, it was the convivial air of the pub that appealed to him. Pubs might have been made to measure for Dylan's satisfaction alone; he fitted into them so snugly. I would go so far as to say that had they served only soft drinks in pubs, Dylan would have been happy—well, almost. More than the alcoholic content of the drink, he would have missed feeling such a devil, drinking the forbidden thing. And had perchance the boot

been on the other foot, had I been snatched away and Dylan
left behind to bear the brunt of gathering age and alcoholism,
I am sure he would have been capable, had he been compelled
to, of settling down almost as happily in total abstinence. He
could adjust to almost any adverse circumstances, though
doubtless he would have missed the pubs terribly. He had a
happier character than mine, by far, and a great gift for making the most of things, however miserable they were. Wherever two or three people were gathered together anywhere—
with or without drink, it made no odds—when Dylan was
there, the spirit of laughter was there.

He lacked the healthy hostility necessary for survival. I
made up for him in that respect. I bristled with hostility. I
wanted to hit everybody new we met because I was afraid of
them and I presupposed, not without reason, that they would
not like me. I was dying to be nice and to be liked, but I don't
think I went about it the right way. A ringing smack in the face
after a few boostering-up drinks was not the best approach. I
only meant to establish contact with them, but it was the
wrong way, I gathered to my dismay, as people started backing
away from me. So, naturally enough, people liked Dylan, even
before he was famous, better than they liked me because
he was more likeable and made them laugh. And I could never
see what there was to laugh about so much. Life, even
then, did not seem to me to be all that bloody funny. I
was never satisfied! I always wanted more. I called it the
divine discontent of the artist, but it was more like the
grumbling discontent of the fisherman's wife in Grimm's fable
who, even when the fish made her pope, found some cause for
complaint. It was too dull, there was not enough to do, so she
then wanted to be like God, to make the sun and the moon go
up. So, for her presumption, she was banished back to her
vinegar jug. And that is where I have been ever since Dylan
left me behind, banished back to my vinegar jug. If I have not
learnt humility yet, in my vinegar jug, I never will.

Yes, Dylan had a natural joy and love of life as unstemmable as breathing, as unstemmable as a Welshwoman's babble. The drink merely accentuated it. It had nothing to do with alcohol; it was not dependent on alcohol. Dylan could be and very often was just as joyful, if not more so, without it, with only soft fizzy drinks, as he was with it. He had domestic orgies of the purest and simplest joys, such as taking a hot bath with books, boiled sweets, pickled onions, nuts and more fizzy drinks piled up on the tray across the bath. Then steadily adding more hot water to his bath as it got cooler and he lost count of time. He would sit in his bath with the water up to his middle, never dreaming of washing himself, reading consistently, putting out a blind hand for whatever tidbits were nearest. When he was soaked as limp as a sponge and boiled as a lobster, he would call me to soap his back, not from a sudden need for cleanliness, for no other part of his body ever got soaped, but from pure lazy indulgence and babyish pleasure at being soaped like a baby by his tender-as-dynamite wife.

His tender-as-dynamite wife scrubbed the pale delicate skin near clean off his back! If she'd had her own way, she'd have skinned him alive. Nor did she melt with tenderness at the sight of him naked—she could not bear men with their clothes off—with his belly all blown up as fat as a pig and the rest of his diminutive body grotesquely out of proportion, as it had become: huge head, huge belly, tiny tapering-off limbs. Nevertheless, she was fiercely possessive of Dylan's once puny but now bulging body and maliciously gloated to herself that now, surely now, no other woman in the universe could reasonably desire to go to bed with such a repulsive object. Now at last, she was confident, he was her indisputable own. She was wrong of course, as usual.

I am not trying to prove that Dylan did not enjoy drinking. He obviously did so, in sympathetic company if possible. It was an essential factor in his gregarious make-up. Dylan rarely, if ever, drank alone, and then never for long. Wherever he went, in whatever dingy hole in the wall, company appeared alongside him. If there was no sympathetic company at the start, it seemed to spring up from the invisible earth, as the sun draws out spring flowers. He was never, to my knowledge, a secret, silent drinker. His parents were the only ones who disapproved, and he never went near them till he was primed up well and good. The parents knew their lectures would have no effect whatsoever on Dylan, but they had to keep on going through the motions even when they were long past controlling Dylan's actions.

It was not his father who led the anti-drink lectures to Dylan. His father kept out of reproving scenes as much as he possibly could and buried himself under his hat and his books. He had a sneaking liking for the "evil influence" himself—which he drank in disciplined moderation in a different pub from the ones we went to. We could hardly blame him for his social discrimination, both for his sake and for ours. We appreciated his gentlemanly tact. Never had Mummy, as Dylan's father called his wife, seen Daddy, as Dylan's mother called her husband, with a drop too much taken. Never, she ranted on to Dylan, had she seen Daddy the worse for drink. Now Daddy did have some sound reasons to be a secret drinker and Dylan swore to me that he had seen him undeniably with more than a drop too much taken—more than one pint over the permitted three pints a night. But perhaps Mummy, not being guilty herself of any vices—besides talking too much over too many cups of tea—was not so quick to recognize the guilty signs of the secret culprit.

I would not like to give a false, unsympathetic impression of Dylan's mother because she was the most sympathetic, good-natured, cosy person, and all the nicest, warmest, friendliest things in Dylan came directly from his mother. She was, in fact, a female replica of Dylan, with only one insignificant omission: his brains. Those he got from his father, who by nature was a shy retiring man, and who by petty circumstances had become a frustrated, disillusioned, cynical man. It was he who had the sensitive soul of the poet—repressed in Welsh mediocrity. It was he who had done all the spade-work of book-learning—which he lacked the courage to put across into poetry. So he handed the buck to Dylan. And Dylan helped himself freely—it was like a second helping for him—from his father's accumulated food of poetry. And with all the power of his mother's sunny personality, he put it across into poetry. Among the three of them, it could not fail, it was a pushover. Between these two opposite extremes—an ingoing father, who, when he should have spoken out, said nothing, and an outgoing mother, who, if even there was one thing she ought not to have said, automatically said it—willy-nilly, a poet was born. It was a lucky dip. It does not mean that a particular combination of opposites will work every time. They are quite as likely to produce a dud who looks fiendishly like its father and signs its name with a king-sized cross. It is the willy-nilly element that must not be left out of the calculations.

16

The Castration of Dylan
as a Poet in America

Sex, violence and drink: the three were inextricably inter-
mingled in my mind. I could not envisage one of these ele-
ments without the other two. They were dependent, all three
of them, one upon the other. I was sure of their order of
importance: drink, violence and sex. There is no doubt in my
mind that sex was my greatest enemy. And it was sex that my
beast desired to kill. Not the funny provocation of a man I
hurled myself upon. He was but the salesman of sex. By cas-
trating him, by taking possession of his sex, I annulled the
threat of weakness. At some past undiggable-up time or
other, sex had obviously made me suffer too much in the
most vulnerable tender folds of my woman's vanity and I was
wreaking my spiteful vengeance upon it. Then, at that blinded
time, I imagined sex as a weapon, as a medal to be won, as
another leaf to be added to my crown of laurels. I treated sex as
a man is said to treat sex. I took my pleasure, so-called, where I
found it, then forgot all about the negligible experience right

away, as though it had never happened.

If I put my mind to a thing, I went about it with a perfectionist's zeal: the perfectionism of the artist in me, I flattered myself. (I did not know then about the perfectionism of the alcoholic in me. Nor would I have admitted to the possibility of such an outlandish idea.) I imagined that I would impress Dylan by showing him that a little provincial boy like him had caught such a gaudy bird. I fancied that by showing him how attractive I was to other men, he would appreciate more jealously his shining catch. My value would be augmented instead of, as curiously enough happened, being decreased. But above all, and this was the rind, core and pips of the matter, I imagined that after seeing with his own two bulging eyes what I could do to him, if he pushed me to do so, he would not dare to betray me himself. But, to my grave disappointment, he hardly seemed aware of my flagrant exhibitions.

My mother's conditioning—for poor mothers are automatically blamed for all their offspring's sins—was largely to blame for my immoral attitude towards sex. Her invariable panacea for all ills, from a suicidal depression to a common cold, was to say lightly, with icy conviction in her unpardonable frivolity: "Why don't you take a lover, dear?"

I could forgive Dylan anything in the line of eccentric madness in his boozy role as the mad excessive poet except for his going with other women. That, for me, was his heinous unforgivable crime. It was a slap in the face to my supreme woman's dominance over him. A whiplash, a crack of the whip to my stinging pride. I was bitterly mortified. I could not accept his fake Don Juan role. It was positively farcical: definitely not his province. He might as well have set himself up as the greatest dancer of the age or I, with the likes of him beside me, set myself up as an immortal poetess.

When his patronesses (they were invariably females!) laid themselves out at his tiny feet in various poetic frenzies, even Dylan could not help but see how absurdly comic it was for him, for his incongruously unsuitable person to be called upon to pay the nominal blood money. But it was the done thing, and Dylan was always a most adaptable and obliging person, particularly when mellowed by drink. So, I suppose, though I could have sworn it was against his natural inclination, he bravely paid the price and gave them the fleeting satisfaction of possessing his sacred container of poetry for an hour or so.

Dylan and I would joke together about his over-ardent patronesses, whose ardour did not stop at poetry. In my presence, he would shudder with reptilian repugnance at the prospect of some forthcoming business encounter with one of these patronesses. To judge by the looks of him afterwards, a bundle of spent, dejected, ragged nerves, the encounters must have been suffocating ordeals for him. The interminable boredom alone of pretending to listen to their interpretations of his poems (the thing he avoided most even from a man) must have been a truly heroic sacrifice on his part.

On Dylan, I always thought, the role of the mock swashbuckling lover sat ridiculously askew. It was thrust on him almost against his will both by the permissiveness of drinking circumstances and the pushiness of females hunting after a famous name. They did not see the man at all. They were bedazzled by the promise of the name.

Certainly it was against his sober character. Sober, he would never have played the mock-Casanova. Nor, sober, would I ever have played the mock-Isadora at her courtesan worst. But then, whatever I did, I could never keep up with Dylan: all the odds were against me, try as I might.

A little glimmering of awareness in a wife is much more detrimental to her peace of mind than none at all. With none at all she can be put out quite happily to grass, there to vegetate and chew her cud till her stud feels the seasonal urge to reproduce himself again. But what writer's wretched wife has not tried, by one desperate means or another, to keep her end up? And almost always failed dismally.

I made the big mistake at the start, the very big mistake, of presuming that Dylan was mine only, bodily mine: that all his bodily hulk, if nothing else, belonged categorically to me for all time. I did not mind sharing his brain but I strongly objected to sharing his body. I believed in my blindness that he was my chosen, made especially for me; my funny, cuddly, softly endearing precious possession whom nobody but myself would be so cracked as to think of choosing for a bed-mate forever.

I have always disliked sharing things. I love giving away things, all my possessions if necessary, but sharing goes deeply against the grain in me. I had bargained that no other woman in her senses could covet the bodily possession of my sympa-thetic little ugly duckling. I felt absolutely safe and secure in that assumption. But, how wrong could I be! How naïve! How puerile to the point of idiocy! On the contrary, it appeared that every woman coveted the bodily possession of my sympathetic ugly little duckling—just to say she had been to bed with a genius for a night. Nobody had told me what the rules of life were in the world of sophistication. But it sank in eventually that to a calculating woman the body is not a joyful plaything but a means to an end. It is to her but a use-ful vehicle to transport her to the name of the brains that made the name. It is not the brains in themselves—they are much too horribly boring—that she is after. It is purely the name—the glamour of the name in association with her own insignificant one—that she is after. As though the bigness of the name would make her own eternal smallness bigger. Brains with no famous name attached to them are so much dust to her.

I understood only very much later on, as Dylan belonged less and less to me and more and more to everybody, that it had to be that way. It was Dylan's destiny to become more and more nobody. When one of two people who once clung close together becomes famous, the other one sinks automatically into obscurity.

Fame brings inexorable estrangement. However hard, however pathetically they both pretend that their love for each other is still the same, it is not. It cannot be. The framework that once held their love together has changed, and their love falls apart.

Our love was born in the framework of adversity, and it flourished no more in the framework of Dylan's success. Notwithstanding that in his success he still lived the life of a drunken pauper because it was the life that suited him best. But there were too many harpies constantly hanging around him for me to be able to tackle the lot single-handed. Worst of all—as the heavy price of fame—while verbally despising the bloody harpies to me, he only too obviously enjoyed their flattery.

It is a bitter, bitter blow for the one who is left behind: nearly always the godforsaken female is left with all her mate's vices and none of his gifts. Like losing her children when they grow up and quietly go off, leaving an unfillable hole, the loss is inexorable—an unchangeable fact. There is nothing she can do about it; no good pretending it is not a fact; no good pretending it is a funny fact. It is not a bit funny; it is a wholly horrible fact. My heart shrank back into itself and I shrank back into our beastly solitary bogs to brood venomously on the unfairness of our split fates: Dylan's to world renown, mine to anonymity. It was a cut deep down to its black bleeding core. Bleeding black drops of blood that fed on themselves and bled more black drops of blood. Dropping black blood into my brain until it was filled to the brim with the hurt of black blood.

Although Dylan howled against continually being in the public eye, nothing on earth would have stopped him going back for more. Let me be brave and face it: it is a hell of a lot more fun being famous than being not famous. Everybody privately or secretly must want to be famous. I am sure of it. Just think of the money: wads of lovely crackling cracklers to do with just as one pleases. To be famous is to be given a prominent identity as opposed to a private one. It is to be made into a sacred untouchable object with limitless permission to do as one sees fit. Is it not preferable to being an unidentifiable member of the masses? Do not listen to the famous ones when they lament about the glut of publicity and their lack of private lives. Nobody is forcing them to be public figures: they are enjoying it, and they could easily get out from on top should they so desire. Famous people, though they like to put on an act of nostalgic longing for private lives, know, in their secret pockets of self-knowledge, that private lives, more often than not, are like lonely beaches that we search for and hope not to find: grey, dreary and oppressive.

Dylan succeeded in public for a very simple reason: he was the "goods"; he had the goods to deliver, and he delivered them. What happened in between delivering the goods was of no importance. A great poet can break with equanimity all the conventional rules of ordinary people. Not only can but must. He is expected to. Ordinary people are disappointed if he does not; he has got to show that he is highly different from themselves. And Dylan always obliged them with highly different and sometimes highly shocking behaviour.

For the alcoholic artist, fame and money together are the most dangerous combination there is, and to resist their combined negative influence he needs to be a superman. The artist in him will never work again and the alcoholic in him will drink himself to death. It has happened over and over again to bedevilled artists. There is no hope of getting any serious work done because he is having too much fun. And having fun is the most insidious deflator of the drive to work. For the artist does not work voluntarily. It is much too uncomfortable a business to begin voluntarily. He has to be driven to work, as a horse is driven out of its comfortable stable. And look how that same stubborn reluctant horse, when turned around, gallops joyfully back again full steam ahead to its comfortable stable. So does the alcoholic artist gallop joyfully back again full steam ahead to his comfortable evasion of work in adulation and intoxication. So did Dylan and it was fatal for him too.

Don't get me wrong. I wanted Dylan's success, but I did not want the vilely disagreeable things that went with it: his inevitable estrangement from me and the ever-expanding pack of predatory women pursuing him. And I wanted my success in the dancing world. I didn't want much, did I? I wanted Dylan's success in the poetic art and my success in the plastic art.

Instead I was left in the embarrassing position of having to reconcile Dylan's uproarious success in America with my hidden insignificance. I was filled with concentrated rancour and tore at the flesh and bit deeper into the bleeding quick of my nails. Failure was a word I was afraid to say, let alone accept. My real terror was resignation to my defeat. I knew how to do nothing in the house, none of the domestic things that most normal women learn as they are growing up. I thought that proved that I must be different, set apart, meant for "better things" than being the abandoned housewife of a famous poet. Even when I was not abandoned, the very term "housewife," as applied to me, made me squirm with disgust. The secondary role of shining in the reflected glory of my husband was definitely not made for me, did not suit me one bit. It was as pallidly insipid as the poor moon's extinction when the sun was up. Like the moon, I had to wait till the sun went down before I could shine all alone.

Around the time of his success in America, Dylan had acquired a new, wealthy Welsh patroness: Marged Howard Stepney. She was a tall, slender woman, approaching middle-age, but still attractive. She was always the perfect lady, except for one little carefully concealed defect: when she came slumming with us she got discreetly drunk and was compelled to stay the night with us. She always brought with her a jolly fat lady (who, we later discovered, turned out to be her keeper) and a suitcase of gin: not to hand around to any of us but to keep beneath her bed for intermittent nips during the night.

Often very late at night, she would ring up Dylan when he was on the point of dropping off to sleep, comfortably tucked up with me in our big bed. He would have to drag himself to the phone and have interminable, drivelling, muttering and murmuring chats with her. I strained my ears to catch what they were saying but never could. I bit my nails to the quick, fumed impotently and whipped myself into a fury of indignation, but for some unknown reason I could never bring myself to get out of bed and shout abuse at them. It seemed to me then that Dylan no longer belonged to me; he was no longer in my territory and was out of my jurisdiction.

When Dylan, after what seemed to me hours of sleepily doling out blood money, came back to bed utterly exhausted and good for nothing, his hackneyed excuse was that he had to be nice and polite since she had promised him vast sums of money to keep us going in the vague hereafter. "In the vague hereafter" were the suspicious words; they were conveniently unclear and had a habit of seldom materializing.

Once, but only once, we were invited to her very grand house. During the evening, she and Dylan became so drunk and sloppily absorbed in each other that I was totally excluded from their nauseating scene. I was drunk too, of course, resentfully so and, at some unendurable moment, I blew my top. I took hold of a very heavy torch from the marble mantelpiece and hit Dylan hard over the head with it. Some archaic prohibition stopped me hitting the lady too, though frankly, I should have much preferred doing so. Dylan did not say anything because he was in no condition to do so. This quiet refined gentle lady, on the other hand, had plenty to say. She turned on me like a cornered rat protecting its young and went for me verbally tooth and nail. She delivered a bristling spiel on the criminality of endangering the brains of a genius. She was right in principle, I had to admit, and I felt terribly remorseful afterwards, though I would sooner have died than let her know. Nevertheless, I had been very severely provoked by both of them and I was out of control, so I think my reaction, though most certainly not right, was most understandable.

Dylan, incidentally, was none the worse for the torch bashing. In fact, he was perfectly unaware of having been hit at all. He must have been happily unconscious for a brief dazed spell. Soon after this unpleasant scene we all retired dejectedly to bed. We were never invited to her grand house again, I am glad to say. Such abused luxury takes weeks of frugal living to recover from.

I never resent spending too much money or having too much money spent on me. But to spend it on things that make one more miserable than one was is nothing less than plain insanity. It is a wicked waste of all the good enjoyable things one could have done with the same amount of money if only one had had it to oneself. This is exactly how I felt after the lavish hospitality of our excessively kind and classically crackpot hostess. She was so obviously deeply unhappy herself. Not the least of her unhappiness was the fact that she was dying to have a baby, but was unable to conceive.

I had been through several miscarriages and abortions in the first few months of pregnancy and was so fighting fit at that early stage that I hardly noticed them. But my most recent pregnancy was the more significant because I was already four months pregnant and because it made it incumbent upon me to make the big decision.

The big decision was whether to get the abortion done, so late in the day, and go with Dylan on his next visit to America, or not to get the abortion and therefore not to be able to go with him.

Marged begged me to keep my pregnancy, but, though I

hesitated over and over, her pleadings were not so powerful as the commanding voice of New York. In my fertile orchard, babies grew like apples on trees, and the problem with us, in our reduced circumstances, was not so much to make babies grow up as it was to keep them down before they ever saw the light of day. Once born there was no pushing them back in again.

It was the thought that I might be missing something more thrilling where Dylan was that was roughly my not-very-praiseworthy motive for dropping everything. I would park out at random my three still very young children with different people, get the operation done post-haste and follow in Dylan's revels, like the fool I was, to my own diminishment. That was the crude truth of the matter. I did not want to be left out of things. And our disappointed new patroness had regretfully to fork out the hundred pounds (which was a lot of money in those days and a fabulous sum for us) for a professional illegal operation for me.

As was my custom, when faced with any traumatic experience, I went through it dead drunk and, in this case, late at night. But the drunkenness, as usual, wore off all too soon and did not prevent me seeing, through an insufficient fog, scraps and chunks of my premature baby being callously chucked into a nearby pail. I kept asking the doctor and his assistant what sex it had been, but they pretended not to hear me and totally ignored my cries.

It was no joke for a woman fundamentally as prudish as I was to be made to strip completely from the waist down and to lie down on the rubber-sheeted surgical bed, with a nurse at the head of it to hold her upper half down. Then to have her ankles tightly strapped into two iron clamps set wide apart on either side of the surgical bed: leaving her thighs wide apart to the mercies of the surgeon. Then to have his hard hands in rubber gloves dig around inside her; to have his shining metal instruments follow suit, coldly probing inside and tugging at nameless chunks of flesh none too gently. To face such an ordeal one needs to be stoned out of one's mind in order that unconsciousness takes the place of an anaesthetic (they were afraid to use it lest the patient die under anaesthesia). Anaesthetic was the one and only thing that Dylan supplied in quantity: in double doses of fiery spirits in the pub opposite this clandestine haunt. To keep up my morale, he gaily explained. That was the last I saw of him on that memorable night. Since Dylan was much too squeamish to accompany me himself, I always had to undergo these backroom indecencies completely alone. I took it for granted then. I accepted his negligence as a matter of course. It was all part of the great British stiff-upper-lipped teeth-gritting code, whereby the men do not soft-soap their wives, and public demonstrations of affection towards them are severely frowned on. Definitely "not cricket," old boy!

After this last significant abortion of mine was all over, I was made to stay the night in that same gruesome establishment. The next morning I felt as lively as a cricket, hopping mad to be off in the open air. My first instinct, once let outside, was to ring up my benefactress, who had so generously paid for the whole business, to tell her all went well and I was feeling fine. I did so only to hear, to my incredulous mortification, from a whispering voice at the other end of the wire, that she had died that very night while sitting up in a chair waiting to hear from me. I was dumbfounded!

There was only one lesson that I could glean from this incredible piece of news. It was that I had been wrong—yet again—to get the abortion done.

It is perfectly true that Dylan and I could not afford another baby—we could not afford the three children we had already—but this provident calculation did not come into the argument with us in any way whatsoever, not in any shape or form. So it is no good using it as a blatantly false excuse.

And when we did at last get away together in January

1952 for our near-fatal visit to America, our three children were parked out haphazardly over the countryside, with scarce regard, on our part, for their general welfare. They were left to sink or swim in the famous public-school system. All in all I think one can safely say that my maternal dedication, though passionate, did leave something to be desired.

As soon as I got to New York, that hypothetically thrilling place, the thrill was abruptly cut short as though an unexploded bomb had dropped on the revellings or, to be exact, as though an unexploded wife had been dropped.

Dylan was still able then to keep most of his appointments and to speak. It took a bellyful of booze to make him speechless. His legs went before his voice; the voice was the last thing to go. He mostly managed, by prudently taking only a few fizzy beers before the event, to do brilliantly inspired readings.

I, on the other hand, had no role to play. I realize now that I cramped his style badly. I followed blindly in his drinking tracks, abortively fighting off the fawning matriarchs hanging onto him in ever-increasing droves. It was understood between us that Dylan was the brains and I was the body. But over there, in that vastly nonsensical place, Dylan, all of a sudden, had become the body as well as the brains. His dogsbody had become the body of the season to go to bed with—while not a dead cat looked at my body which I had worked on so hard. Nor was I given the compensation of brains to fall back on. There were too many bloody women to compete with.

It was a losing battle from the start. I saw it, but I could not bring myself to relinquish Dylan passively into their grabbing hands. I went on fighting for him when I knew it was all no good. I had not a beggar's chance of winning. They were too numerous and one of them always had her painted claws in him.

Towards the end of his life, there were no more "Love you Forevers" from Dylan. He was too busy in America, pretending to become the great adulterer. This last pitifully ridiculous Casanova role, which nobody could have fitted less suitably than Dylan, was foisted upon him and was anathema to me: the final insult. It put both Dylan and me to shame and took away all the dignity in our love. It killed our faith in each other. It was an unforgivable thing to do.

Dylan would never have admitted to me, nor I think to anybody else, that our love was anything less than perfect, or that he was far better off in America without me: unhampered by a megalomaniac wife. Before setting off again on his compulsive voyages of destruction, he would plead with me to go back with him as though he desperately needed me. And I do believe he thought he did: he was both terrorized and fascinated by America. I could not help being carried away by the sincerity of his words—and I began believing him all over again. Fat fool I was—didn't I know it was his job; he could turn it on like a tap to anybody he wanted to inveigle and I fell, melted for it, every time. My pent-up indignation and bitterness against him ebbed out of me and a high tide of reciprocal love and joy surged back into me.

Dylan needed to be alone in America to have full unrestricted scope; to have enough rope to do all he needed to do, all the good and the bad things a great poet has got to do, in order to make his legend live in his lifetime. He had an unfailing sense of dramatic timing: had he not died just when he did, on his last visit to America alone, his great poet's legend would not have been half so dramatic.

I could see his point. What would have happened to his legend of our immortal love if we had gone on nominally together, the two of us, one as bad as the other? It was bound to break up sooner or later if Dylan had not broken himself first: broken away from it to keep it intact. What would a great poet be without his immortal love? Immortal love and early death are the icing on the cake of a great bard.

When Dylan was away from me, over regular intermittent

periods, in Persia, for example, where he was once on some
sort of job connected with the high price of their oil at that
time, it was a lot easier for him to keep up his old legend of
the immortality of our love. He did as he pleased, then he sat
down, wherever he was, and wrote me one of his Specials, his
special star turns, turning on shamelessly the jet of tear-
jerkers. He was adept at rending the hearts of his readers. And
just when I had got to the point of deciding it was all over and
done with between us, that I was never going to hear from
him again (I had no idea where he was staying, no address, no
telephone number), one of his Specials would arrive! One of
his beautiful passionate love letters overflowing with everlasting love for me and gigantic despair at being so long away
from me. Not so gigantic, however, as to make him come
home to me in a hurry or to stop him leaving me on the next
auspicious occasion.

Every creator has this rising fear of losing his sacred sap.
Had Dylan been able to go on quietly and anonymously, as at
the beginning, I believe that he would surely have produced
more and even better stuff. But after his castration as a poet
in America, it was not possible for him to turn back the clock
and start again from scratch. He had produced enough to
make his personality felt and his name heard to the ends of
the earth. He was both a writing poet and a living poet, but
he spent more time being a living poet acting out his personal
legend. As he himself once said, in one of his rare moments of
humility: he was not Shakespeare.

Dylan must have been hurt, I think now, not only by my
completely ignoring his poetic side, but by my positively
pushing it away from me as though I was afraid of being contaminated by it. He must have been hurt, even if he was not
aware of it himself, by my always escaping as fast as I could
from his readings. He never said so to me, nor to anybody
else. I don't think he ever said so to himself. He had already
such a bunch of listeners and admirers. I never thought to

presume he might also need my wifely support. But, who knows, perhaps he did. A wife's support is a different thing. It is a mother's cradling of the creator's head, and the held head of the creator is a large part of his creation. It was perhaps this lack of mental cradling, though our bodies rocked together nightly clutched in each other's arms, that caused him to seek mental support elsewhere, that caused me to lose him. But, if so, it was only one of the minor causes. I knew only too well what the major cause was. It was the malignant power of alcohol destroying us both and destroying our love.

I made my nonparticipation in poetry so obvious in America that when we went to the grand houses of the very rich and the inevitable happened, when they asked Dylan to read them a poem, I insisted upon modestly retiring. I was graciously conducted to a chamber apart, rather like a dentist's waiting room, where I thumbed the tedium away through glossy magazines. Would he never stop, I raged to myself, had he got to choose his longest poems, then another, then another...he was revelling in it too, there was no doubt about that. Until at last he had done, and I could reappear, all radiant and uncontaminated, to pounce on and guzzle a colossal bourbon on the rocks graciously waiting for me.

Dylan's homecomings from America, more dead than alive, must have been a frightful anticlimax for him. What he needed was rest and quiet, peace and silence. But what he got were more parties and celebrations with his old friends.

Dylan was not the type to turn back, to change, to cure himself. He did not want to be cured. To his wishful way of thinking, there was nothing wrong with his life. He enjoyed it tremendously, so long as his body allowed him to. Until he collapsed physically from the bludgeonings of drink. And only then, in acute sickness, when he had no choice left but to retire from the broad and easy joys of destruction to the straight and narrow joys of creation, would he return home. His physical forces could not keep up with his mental forces, which may have been just as well, may have been his saving as a poet. Nothing would stop him setting forth again, once he was feeling slightly more himself, for his next onslaught—ostensibly money for us—into the enemy territory of his city-drinking friends who were the most pernicious enemies of would-be money-making creators. His drinking friends represented to him a steep precipice which he could do no less than hurl himself over, arse over tip.

Dylan would never have had the patience or tenacity to turn back. It was not his swigging style. Once launched into the fatalistic way of life of the suicide gang, there was no retreat. He was going to drink to his own suicide—all in one gulp—down to its inglorious acid dregs—if it killed him. As it ingloriously did, with the acid dregs of his asinine suicide.

He would never have admitted the inadequacy of his home life or of me as his wife. For Dylan, his wife and his home embodied an untouchable sanctuary, one that he seldom touched. But we still kept up a great show of love. We tried to ignore that great gulf of experience that had made of Dylan (without his wishing it upon himself) a different person, but it was impossible to ignore. He was an estranged person. No longer mine! A sadder person, it seemed to me, or was it only my own sadness at seeing and pretending not to see that he was lost to me? It seemed that we had lost, never to recapture, our first innocent love.

Something irrevocable had happened. As we clung together desperately, for dear life, we might as well have been clinging to a stuffed dummy of the other, for all the good that was in it. Anybody else would have done just as well, if not better, as a bed-cuddler and a warming pan. A drinker is not choosy of his bed companions: he makes them up as he fucks along. For him, all bodies become approximately one.

It was all falling: falling into each other's arms; falling down in drink, and eventually, at the dark end of the blacked-out evening, falling into the nearest bed at some long-suffering friend's house, on top of each other. We were both of us love-shy, except in drink. And it is a pity we were not a bit more love-shy in drink. We loved to visualize ourselves as the all-conquering lovers of the age when, in reality, we were anything but. In reality the battleground of love and sex was a fearsome thing that we could tackle only in drink—and fled from in sobriety. That sex caused such a mountain of bitter blood between us is now inconceivable. Yet it did. It plagued our lives.

When, some time later on, we got back home to our waiting penitentiary that I had flown from so exuberantly to meet Dylan, we both had to recuperate from our joint orgiastic reunion. But Dylan always behaved impeccably at home; he was much too weakened to behave otherwise. Like the perfect little gent that the credulous people down there always said he was. Of me the credulous people down there could not, with all the credulity in the world, say that I was always the perfect little lady. Having seen in Dylan's lengthy absences my frantic carryings-on, my brawling on the floor of the bars, as though by out-scandalising him I could miraculously catch up with him. So they said, with tight-lipped resignation, they would have to shoot her. And they loudly lamented that such a nice little gentleman as Dylan should have been so cursed with such a malediction of a wife.

They were right—with the righteousness of a herd of animals smelling where the grub is. Dylan was basically a piece of bread eaten up by the vultures. And I was one of those vultures. It is not true that you can't keep a good woman down. You can. But it is true that you can't keep a bad woman down. They have not shot me yet.

When I was in America with Dylan and we were drinking nonstop and the vulture women were hunting him down in their flocks, snatching him away from me right and left, I simply stood by, rooted to the spot, and watched it happen. An extraordinary transformation had taken place in me. To my horror, I no longer felt the justified possessor of Dylan, defending indignantly my rights of possession. Instead I felt like an intruder on foreign ground, where Dylan belonged more to all of them than he did to me. Where I was the upstart, the impotent outsider whose prior claim to Dylan was void and whose standing in their land was nonexistent. At the crude abduction scenes of Dylan under my very eyes I found myself retiring discreetly into the background—as though it was I who had committed a terrible error of bad taste by witnessing them, by being there at all. I was made to feel by the vulgar aggressors who had usurped my place that I was very small. At home I would have felled at a blow any such abominable transgressors of the holy bonds of matrimony.

There is no getting away from it; Dylan was very weak in all affairs of the flesh. He followed the commands of these overpowering women like a mesmerized mouse diving down the throat of a cobra. I am not saying he had no enjoyment in the process; it was flattering to his vanity, if no more. And I was weak too, over there, and like a mesmerized mouse watching it all going on, in that too permissive environment. There was nothing, so far as I could see, that was not permitted. Since there were no limits to liberty of action, I lost my strength to protest. I was a shuddering maiden aunt of disapproval. But the real weakness was not so much in our original characters, but above all in the effects of continuous alcohol. Nothing mattered any more. Nothing had any more value. Not a soul, it seemed after a time, could have cared less what we did with ourselves—two immigrant mice from faraway Wales.

It was I, not the poet, who wandered lonely as a cloud in America and beheld a host of golden Americans. But there was no gold in it for me—bar the gold of rye on the rocks. They are so unbelievably kind at the start and so believably fickle at the last. To Dylan, the ladies of America sent flowers…

In the midst of this fool's paradise of self-delusion for Dylan (for me it was a fool's inferno of self-delusion), Dylan was still as sweet as honey to me in words and gestures. He still insisted that I was the most supreme, the most unique, the most beautiful woman in the world, that I was his one and only solitary immortal love forever. And I think, even now, that he seriously meant it. He deceived himself even more than he deceived me, if that was possible. There was never a nasty word out of him that I can recall, never a nasty gesture towards me. Never, least of all, a frank admittance that he ever had been with another woman. That he could ever prefer or ever had preferred another woman to me was inadmissible for him. He stoutly denied to the bitter end, even in the face of incontrovertible proof to the contrary, that he would ever dream of going with another woman. Maybe he would never have dreamt of it. Maybe he just did it and dreamt that it was me. Self-delusion is a very useful cover-up for a blatantly false statement.

If true love is truly wishing for the true good of the loved one—to the point of letting them live with another love if that person was their true good—then, I am afraid, neither of us had ever possessed it. We were both of us much too old-fashioned—prudish and moral at heart—to have even permitted such an outrage of emancipation. We could do it privately, in drink, but never permit it openly in sobriety. Each one of us thought we had this prerogative—since it meant nothing to us—but that the other one had not. The other one of us had to be a monument of fidelity. The result was that when away from each other we both betrayed the other flagrantly, and then swore when we were together again that we did not. This was our one and eternal conflict, because neither of us could be absolutely certain of the other one's good faith. Everybody but us saw what each was doing to the other. But most of them did not like to say so. They did not like to spoil our fairy tale of true love. With typical British reticence, they shut an eye and let us go on bluffing ourselves and each other. So we kept it up for as long as we could until it was useless to bluff any more, until the pile of evidence, the pile of fornicating bodies between us, was too high.

I am certain now that this was the provocation for our violent physical fights in the night. They were my fights, not Dylan's, driven by drink and by his infidelities working on me in a furious unison. I attacked him and he attempted to defend himself like a small fuzzy ball, like a soft hedgehog, his head going bump-bump-bump on the floorboards. It was a wonder there were any brains left in it. In the morning it was just the same as it always was with us in the morning. We were hung-over but tenderly loving. Extra tenderly loving to make up for that black tempest of the night before that was fast-fading into a nightmare that had never happened, that we very soon forgot all about. My first question in the morning was always: "What did I do awful last night?" But it was a joking question and it got a joking answer: "Oh, you only smashed up the whole joint at so-and-so's. We can't go there again." As though it were no more than an amusing anecdote of no concern to anybody, no more than an ordinary everyday happening in our ordinary everyday lives. But for some strange reason our night-fights were never mentioned by us in the morning. Perhaps we both felt afraid that there were deeper, frightening reasons for them and we did not care to talk about them. Then, as the day wore on, and the drink did its dirty work, the devil got into us again and his old volcano of destruction started erupting in us, just like the night before.

But what were we really like underneath the alcohol? What was the whole truth about us? The truth is that I have not got a glimmering of a clue. And I still cannot get at it—not the whole truth, only little bits, stray fragments that emerge out of an impenetrable barrier of alcohol. It could be that our hearts were eaten up by alcohol and simultaneously fed on alcohol. It could be that if alcohol had been suddenly removed from our lives there would have remained precious little of our famous hearts. It could be that they were a pure invention of alcohol. I have a horrible suspicion that alcohol invented them and alcohol kept them pepped up, that they were the glowing offspring of alcohol. We know that alcohol is allergic to the truth, and in that allergy lies its charm.

If only I still had my written answers to Dylan's beautiful loving letters to me, most of which were sent back in his jumbled-up suitcase from America, I would have now at least an indication of how I felt then, and of how I expressed myself in those dark ages past. As things are, I am a baffled stranger to my long-ago enigmatic person, totally unconnected, it seems, to the person I am now. Alas, Dylan's mother, in terror of what the neighbours would have thought, destroyed all my letters to Dylan after his death. So now I have nothing to go on but tentative guessing and the feeling that the beautiful corn-coloured girl of Dylan's love letters had nothing to do with me. The real me is not a separate entity: it is an accumulation of separate parts, each one equally real when it is being acted upon. Likewise Dylan's beautiful corn-coloured girl lived in his corn-coloured fancy, in his romantic unreality. She was real to him, but not to me. I may have looked the part, but I did not feel the part: there was no corn-coloured girl in my oyster-closed heart.

Dylan's love letters were too much like his poems, intimately personal, yet they did not apply to me. He laid it on just a wee bit too thick, like strawberry jam. I may be horribly suspicious again, but I can't help feeling that they could have been written, with equal passion, to any other blonde bitch. It was his verbal passion that was important—not the ungrateful reaction of his blonde bitch. I was given a genius poet who loved me passionately and I have the nerve to complain that he put too much jam on it. Some people are never satisfied! My only importance to the world was in my connection with Dylan. And though I should have been content simply to be Dylan's chosen "moll," I was not. There were altogether too many chosen molls in America.

17
Madness Is a Convenient
Escape from Responsibility

It all happened so fast—it seemed, in the first few seconds after my arrival at the hospital in New York. My first night in New York after Dylan's collapse (on November 5, 1953) was spent in a disgusting bin, brutally laced in a straitjacket. I was in a horrible confusion, with the fogging of whisky on top of my scrambling emotions, scrambling to get out from under the fog.

Certain disjointed particulars stuck out painfully, but they did not join up into any logical sequence of events. I remembered being hustled from the plane, already drunk, into the hospital room where Dylan lay half under an oxygen tent, with drips going into one arm. I did not know what to do, so I sat down heavily on the edge of his bed and started to try to roll a cigarette. But the tobacco fell out all over the sheets and I gave it up. I was embarrassed by the rows of gazing faces. All his friends had gathered on the other side of the glass partition at the side of the room. They had been watching and waiting for days before I came over. And I remembered then that Dylan's latest girlfriend was surely among them, devoutly watching and waiting over him too.

A surge of rage leapt up in me, and I vowed if it was the last thing I did, I was going to kill that self-possessed girlfriend. It was not Dylan I was thinking of on his deathbed, it was the annihilation of that hypocritical woman behind the glass, who did all the right things at the right times and who made me sick. Realizing that something more was expected of me in this last dramatic deathbed scene, I got up bodily on top of what there was of Dylan protruding from his oxygen tent to transmit some of my raging alcoholic life into his reluctantly breathing frame. While I was lurching about on top of him, I saw his little frail fish-hand lying there beside us, the same little frail fish-hand with which he had dared to touch other women. I touched it, and held it hard with my square, stump-fingered hand. I wanted to be the ultimate one to stake my physical claim on him. The rest of those self-possessed whores could have his writing to masturbate over for the rest of their putrid lives. His hand was as warm as his words would have been could he have felt and seen me there, wobbling about on top of him. He would have enjoyed it, he would have been amused. But the white-coated people said I was stopping him breathing and they pulled me off him.

I was outside the glass partition now, with the others, gazing in, and I was banging my head against the glass and howling. Some part of my brain noted how well I was playing the scene, and told me to keep it up.

At another indeterminate point, later on, I don't know how I got there, I was in a large empty hospital ward. I was hanging upside-down, high up, very high up out of reach, with my knees crooked over the bars that had been pulled up near to the ceiling. I was doing a very skilful acrobatic act between the bars that divided the empty beds. I was travelling, high up, upside-down, with my head hanging down, from one set of bars to the next, all round the large empty ward. I was up there a very long time, and I began to worry, would nobody ever take any notice of me and come to fetch me down? Somebody, some more white-coated people I suppose, must have come at the end and must have got me down somehow. But my strength must have been too much for them. My strength, in the condition I was in, would brook no restraint. It was enormous; it could bend bars.

With no transition, I was somewhere below stairs, in something like a hall, and I was facing a man-sized wooden crucifix, fixed in an alcove in the wall. It was, I dimly registered, Saint Vincent's Hospital that Dylan was in. "I will show those buggers what I think of their Christ," I raged, and I strove mightily to tear their crucifix away from the wall and out of its alcove. I think I tore it clear out of its alcove and I think I broke it on the floor. But one should not boast.

It must have been then, at this last outrage, that the white-coated people truly turned on me in their numbers, and gave me what I deserved, what I had been asking for all along, to be put away, along with Dylan. Why should he be allowed to be put away, and not me? And me be left out in the cold? Why should he always get all the favours and me none? It was not cricket, and Dylan was always so keen on cricket. I had asked for internment too, and I had got it. And I could not even blame those unfortunate white-coated people who had given it to me. Nobody could say, not even me, that they had not been provoked.

Between sanity and insanity, it is said, there is a very thin line. In my case there was no such tremulous line, I was perfectly sane, nowhere near insanity. But extreme amounts of alcohol can make its subject, the one who is subjected to it, play some very insane tricks. And those tricks can trick the beholders of them into thinking that it is the subject that is insane, when, in fact, it is the alcohol that is making the subject behave insanely. When the subject is sober once

again, it automatically, if unhappily, becomes sane. And this is
what happened to me when I was put in the Bellevue asylum.
I automatically, if unhappily, became sane again. I wish to
God I really was insane like the other lucky ones who did not
know who or where they were. I knew, with an appalling
knowledge, exactly who and where I was.

When I was finally unlaced from my ignominiously stifling restriction, I found myself beating my head and weeping
buckets of tears against the whitewashed walls of the institu-
tion. Before, tears would not come. They were lodged in a
huge gob in my throat, but they came out in this permissive
atmosphere, they poured out uncontrollably. I could not stop
them. Nobody took a bit of notice. All the prisoners cried
there: they went there to have a good cry. Their tears were a
flood of suddenly unleashed pain.

In these recuperating havens one is taught gently but
firmly to restrain all signs of violence in oneself. Or one will
never be let out again. So I remained stonily mute, as though
I had not heard somebody flatly announce (on November 9)
that Dylan was dead.

For me, in any case, Dylan was already dead: had been for
all those artificially prolonged days and nights of re-enforced
breathing and intravenous feeding in the hospital. I knew he
was never going to come out of his pleasurable coma in his
oxygen tent. Dylan always longed to go into a coma. It was the
nearest thing to the womb. Only his failing breath petered out
at last. Thank God. Dylan's agony was done. What was the
point of preserving any longer an already dead man for his
agonizing friends and lovers to gaze at night and day through
the glass partition, hoping, hopelessly, for a miraculous change
in him? Those kinds of miracles do not happen. He was all
there to the naked eye: small as life. Yet none of him, none of
Dylan's true essence, was there at all. None at all, none.

How can one mourn a person when only the shape is
there, as insensible as a log or a tree trunk? With no presence

to wring the tears out, there are no tears. I saw and felt all this at the time, but did not know it and could not say it. I had not learned yet how to mourn: how to be a mourning widow. I have now. I have practised going underground.

All bad and good things have got to come to an apparent end. Although I managed to keep up the high drama for an exceptionally long time, eventually I exhausted myself and my means of livelihood. For us down-and-out Britishers, the British Consulate in New York provided a haven of security when all else failed. It was therefore to the Consul that I went with my request for the fare for my passage home in a boat, with Dylan in his coffin in the hold.

The Consul was courtesy itself. I begged him to book me a cabin *alone*: it was imperative for me in my shattered condition. He reassuringly agreed to do so and solemnly promised to book me one of the best cabins in first class all to myself. He quite understood, he added benignly with a little pat on my shoulder, my distressed state of mind. I could take his solemn word for it. Like a poor innocent trusting lamb, I did. He then called his secretary to walk me up and down in the passageway outside his office: the typical Britisher's panacea to pain.

After the grandiose send-off on the deck with all the friends, flowers and "champers" bubbling round me one minute, then the ship's hooter for departure, then nobody the next, I went down below to bury myself alone in my cabin, which I had not yet seen! It turned out to be a double cabin, and the woman I was to share it with was already there. The last thing I could have put up with was a glamorous lady sitting at *my* dressing-table, gazing entranced at herself and putting on the finishing touches to her enticing embellishment. The contrast between my tearfully bedraggled state and her positively crowing triumph would have been unbearable to me. All I longed for was solitude.

It would take all of my British sterling qualities to weather this punch below the belt. I would take a leaf from the British Consul's book: his gently dissembling book. It would mean my putting on the act. Not again? Yes, again. There was no other way out; I had to get out of sharing that cabin at all costs.

Trust me, I was an old hand at putting on the act. There was only the old "song-and-dance" routine to be got under way. It was really quite simple: I just had to walk into the still-empty bar-room at about five o'clock and order myself *five double whiskies* all at the same time. (I told them I was waiting for my four friends to turn up.) Then, think no more. Let the whiskies take over: just wait patiently. They would not take long to function all on their own. Unlike the British Consul, they could be depended upon to do their stuff.

There was soft suggestive music in the background of the bar-room. My legs and arms moved of their own volition: they shot out in all directions. They picked up screwed-down chairs like feathers, flinging and kicking them flying into the far corners of the bar-room. In one sweeping movement of arms they whisked glasses and ashtrays off tables and shattered them to shining fragments. Legs and arms, in combination, dislodged the dislodgeable tables by themselves, tearing them up at the roots. Between my natural, not inconsiderable physical strength and the undauntable strength of the alcohol, there was no stopping us. I was as strong and ferocious as a lioness defending her cubs: although in this case I was defending my five double whiskies. I was whirling wilder and wilder, riotously high-kicking, crashing down, splitting knife-like on the now-splintered floor, swiping aside, yanking up, every conceivable obstruction littering my full-steam-ahead stampede.

In the middle of my dance of destruction, I blearily noted that the captain of the ship had appeared and was looking at my antics appreciatively, while simultaneously sternly ordering his subordinates to lock me away in the hold. Did I imagine it or had he actually given me a big slobbery, leering wink?

As circumstances proved a bit later on, I had not imagined it.

This turn of events of course was precisely what I had aimed at: to be locked up alone in the hold with Dylan in his "box" beside me. It was really quite comfortable, homely and peaceful down there. Above all, I had shaken off the imposition of an unwished-for companion for my woebegone voyage home. My revolutionary act had achieved its end, which was to make myself so undesirable aboard ship that I had to be put away.

After a couple of days and nights locked up alone in the hold, stewing in my own evil juices, I wrote a little letter of supplication to the captain to let me out again. I was greatly relieved to be summoned by him, and I dolled myself up in my new clothes presented to me by our most generous coloured actor friends in New York.

That night I sat grandly at the captain's table delicately sipping at my strictly prescribed (three only) bourbons on the rocks. I must confess that I felt a complacent satisfaction to nonchalantly observe, from my elevated vantage point, my previously snooty, "magpie lady of my cabin" sitting at a lower-level table gazing up at me in unbelieving and, I swear, envious astonishment!

Such frivolities serve to ward off the big pain of loss, which comes without warning, like the in-rushing tides of the Boat House which never failed to keep their unpredictable appointments and do their drowning duty day after day. They are as unstoppable as death.

I kept waiting for my death! I was more than ready. But Dear Death was not yet ready for me; it had decided to keep me waiting. Dear Death is just like an orgasm that never comes. Then, just when one has given up all hope completely, it comes!

Dear Death is so perverse that it takes the best people first, in the prime of their lives, and leaves alone the refuse people to stew in their own evil juices. In Dear Death's opinion, I had not yet suffered enough punishment for my previous sinful life. In my opinion, I had suffered enough (if not too much already) and I saw no point in going on suffering, unwanted by man or beast, trudging through my days killing time. Unfortunately, I am not the suicidal type. I could never bring myself to deliberately extinguish the flickering light still left in me.

Soon after Dylan died, I went on a mad round of parties. One after the other continuously; the next one madder than the last, as though I was celebrating my glorious freedom, which in a sense I was from—my loony bin. What can the onlookers have thought of my demented behaviour? What can they have thought of my grief, which was so well disguised that it looked more like boundless joy? I drank and drank and drank. There was no limit to my drinking. The greatest thing was never to come to.

Of course we all know that there is nothing more revolting than a drunken or drugged wife, husband, father or mother. It is subtly insinuated that any other drunken lout, who is not a wife or a mother or a parent, is comparatively seductive. Nobody disputes this pitiable declaration: least of all the drunken. But it would be as well for the viceless know-alls to pause, for an iota of their self-righteous time, to consider that it is no pleasure either for the drunk to look at herself the morning after.

She lies flat out and can barely move. The merest little physical necessity is a gigantic effort; and she wishes, from the bottom of her nauseous poison-pit, that she had never been born: longs only for blind annihilation. Alongside her physical malady, her humiliating hangover, comes the grisly old Biblical sense of sin, of guilt and remorse, pumped into her from time immemorial. She hates, despises and reviles the mental picture that ruthlessly confronts her of her last night's elated self. It is like being forced to look into a distorting mirror at the reflection of a disgusting obscene monster, a contaminated bloated toad that cannot bear the sight of itself. Then, on top of her own ignominious blameful misery is heaped blame from the family, blame from the family's friends and blame from the general populace. Gradually upwards she worms her weary way to her re-established seat of impersonal dignity, then precipitately downwards she cascades, in an unthinking twinkling to her all-too-familiar compulsory self-destruction. So overwhelming are the accumulated incoming tides of evil killing waters that she feels that her clean original goodness has been scum-washed away. That, in spite of trying with every tendon, everything has been in vain. She has accomplished less than nothing. She is, in her own undisputed estimation, the hugest flop, failure and deadweight. So what does the now-dotty demented creature do? She does the only thing she can do to make herself feel she still belongs to the human species, contemptible as the human species is. She quietly and deliberately, even secretly, takes a hair of the dog that bit her. That "hair" recreates a necessity for another, then a couple more to round off the first medicinal couple. So that, once again, very soon, the "hairy dog" is plucked bald, and the laboriously reinstated housewife has incongruously sprouted a thick beard of false confidence. Her quaking voice starts to yodel with Swiss courage. Her shaking hand to shake less: the bottle not to clank so loudly against the evasive glass. At any moment, she may be moved to thump either the counter or the table or, with greater gusto, the nearest innocent idiot standing beside her.

The professional sneerers, in their crouched corners, bibbing milk, nipping yoghurt or dipping straws into non-alcoholic fizzy fluids, both hope for and fear of her unpredictable outbursts: hope for their sneering diversion, and fear that they might become the targets of it, that she will pick one of them up bodily, hurl them up in the air, bang them down on the floor and jump joyfully on their prone bodies.

For some considerable time after Dylan died, somebody

had only to bring up his name, quite innocently, and I would hurl myself at him bodily, push him crashing to the ground and punch and pummel him vigorously with all my grief-stricken strength. It was my rather eccentric way of expressing my grief, if indeed it was grief. Now I wonder, was it grief? Or was it that I would have preferred to have my name mentioned?

There was not a lot of true love left over in either of us—after the official dying of Dylan. Not till a lot later on—not till now—at the final summing up, as the rot is falling away, layer upon layer of it—did a tiny root of true love shoot up again unexpectedly, just when I had finally decided with cynical satisfaction that no such thing as true love had ever existed or could ever exist. True love is loving and not wanting to possess the object of that love. But that can only be done, by those who are not saints, when the object is dead and gone. So if one member of a twosome must die in order that their love becomes true love, is it not better that they stick to ordinary human possessive love with all the multitudinous hells that go with it? Or not? It is a debatable question.

But ours was a drink story, not a love story, just like millions of others. Our one and only true love was drink and the only significant difference between our drink story and any of the other drink stories is that in the middle of it was a genius poet. Otherwise nobody would have taken a fragment of notice of it. And I can now safely say, after living with a poet and a bottle and now possessing neither one, I know which one comes first, which one is the most important. No man was ever mourned so long, so dolefully or so dolorously as the contents of the bottle. Mourning a man is a sentimental indulgence. Mourning a bottle is a craving pain. Mourning them both is a crying-out-loud nostalgia for a whole lifetime that is finished and can be no more. Can never come again.

afterword

It is easy to judge my mother, Caitlin Thomas, negatively. Many people have painted her as a wild drunken woman, an almighty Irish fighter, a light-hearted Messalina and an irresponsible and unloving mother. They have described Caitlin's bohemian life with Dylan in a reproving tone and a discrediting light. But these people have underestimated the devastating effects that alcohol can produce on the mind and the body. It is far too easy to criticize and condemn an alcoholic.

It is undeniable that during Caitlin's life with Dylan, alcohol became her tyrant. She lost the values that were most precious to her: her respect for and curiosity about nature, her self-esteem, her health, her passion for dancing, her love for Dylan. Every possible attempt at a normal life failed miserably.

As a reaction to Dylan's death, Caitlin left Laugharne and went to London. There, she was looked after by her sister Nicolette and a close friend, Cordelia Locke. Dylan had died as he had lived—penniless—and a charitable fund had to be opened for his widow and children. Dylan's estate consisted only of literary copyrights, which in 1953 Caitlin entrusted to a London literary agent and some old friends of Dylan's.

It was during Caitlin's London stay in early 1954 that she decided to leave England for Italy. She knew that a "permanent and irrevocable change of air" was necessary to safeguard her mental and physical survival. The past had to be left to simmer; "distraction" was now the operative word in my mother's mind.

When Caitlin came to Italy, wine and strong spirits were still her favourite propellant. They unleashed in her a series of almighty fighting matches, most of which took place in crowded restaurants, in dreary bars or at animated party gatherings. She could knock a man down with the greatest of ease. Normally, a slap across the face would be sufficient. When Caitlin was in a belligerent mood, her favourite attack was a high kick under the man's chin or, if there wasn't enough space, an upper-cut or a painful kick in the man's "tender spot." The results were always rewarding.

On a mid-September evening in 1957, Caitlin and a friend were in Rome at a restaurant not far from Piazza di Spagna called Taverna Margutta, a port of call for artists, actors, musicians, writers, photographers, curious tourists and freaks. The two women went out of curiosity, rather than to eat Italian food. The cosmopolitan atmosphere was also congenial to my father Giuseppe Fazio, then thirty-three years old and fluent in French, German, Spanish and English. At the time he was working as an assistant director and soon became the indispensable *trait d'union* to film companies employing international crews.

Giuseppe and his friends invited the two ladies to join their jolly company. To break the barrier of shyness, Caitlin begun to drink heavily. Giuseppe, shocked by the drinking capacities of the attractive blonde foreigner, suggested she moderate her consumption of alcohol. Caitlin felt reproached like a "little naughty girl" in front of everybody and began insulting Giuseppe and finished by punching him on the nose. Slightly surprised by this reaction, Giuseppe quickly caught Caitlin's wrists and immobilized her. Caitlin's fiery Irish spirit had met Giuseppe's volcanic Sicilian temperament.

Giuseppe had then seen only the tip of the iceberg of Caitlin's alcohol problem. Nor did he understand alcoholism: in his life he had met only a few harmless social drinkers. And he knew nothing of Dylan Thomas's poetry, only that the poet had died recently, leaving Caitlin with three children. Perhaps it was Caitlin's great vulnerability that made Giuseppe take her under his protective wing. Caitlin was then without a companion and virtually alone in "no man's land."

Their relationship was uneasy from the first. It became, all too soon, an endless chain of animated rows. On several occasions Giuseppe rescued Caitlin from suicide attempts. He had no idea how to cope with a belligerent, insulting, argumentative alcoholic, but he knew he had to find a solution.

In 1958 Caitlin was hospitalized in a private clinic for complete detoxification from alcohol. This was followed by many other vain attempts to stay dry.

In the early sixties my mother thought she was pregnant. However, an English gynecologist told her that her bulging belly was due to "hysterical pregnancy" and that there was nothing to worry about. As a result, determined to flatten her indecent growing belly, she intensified her regime of exercises: extra swimming, more horseback riding along the white sandy beaches and longer bicycling expeditions in the midday sun. Meanwhile I was disconsolately bouncing and vaulting in all directions, incarcerated in the pitch dark. No wonder I came out into the world prematurely, upside-down and, wisely, feet first.

Caitlin was so happy at this unexpected gift from God that she made a promise to herself: "If my baby manages to live, I'll give up drinking altogether!" It proved to be not so easy. I was put in an incubator for two months, and obviously survived, but it took a while for Caitlin to face the problem of alcohol.

As a child I suffered greatly from the constant rows between the two people I most loved. Finally in 1973 my mother realized that even if she had a good reason to stop drinking she could not make it alone. She decided to follow my father's advice to join Alcoholics Anonymous and attend meetings three times a week. "Let's give it a try," she told my father. "If it doesn't work, at least I'll have met some new desperate cranks like myself."

He joined Al-Anon (a support group for families of

alcoholics) and also went to meetings three times a week. This routine continued for more than ten years.

For the first three years my mother was completely mute at the Alcoholics Anonymous meetings. Nevertheless, she kept going. Realizing that her inborn shyness could perhaps be mitigated if she put down her thoughts on paper and read them aloud, she started writing about her experiences with alcohol and Dylan. Writing helped, as did listening to the confessions of recovered alcoholics. Slowly the healing effects of understanding and solidarity from other sufferers percolated through Caitlin's shield of protection.

It was hard for Caitlin to create new occupations to take the place of the old, embedded, harmful habits. Nature proved useful to her since it kept her mind off drink, and was a reminder of her joyful childhood. As part of the healing process, she followed with great discipline an "open-air therapy program," which included walking expeditions in most of Rome's parks, bicycling, horseback riding, swimming and late-evening window-shopping.

Then came the problem of finding an innocuous substitute for wine. A mix of fresh blood-red oranges and German grape juice became her new cocktail. Her body required great quantities of iron and vitamin B so each night we both had a healthy bowl of chopped-up fruit, together with white yogurt, fresh liquid yeast, wheat kernels and plenty of honey. In the daytime she drank the juice of freshly squeezed spinach, carrots, parsley, celery and tomatoes.

She made up for lost time. She became interested in the lives and works of the great writers, painters, sculptors and explorers. Together, we visited many art galleries, museums and architecture exhibitions, but above all she liked going into churches to absorb the atmosphere.

When she was sixty-five, my mother taught me to dance. When she was seventy, I used to take her on the back seat of my scooter to her swimming lessons or to the park to play badminton. Outdoor activities, plenty of work and self-discipline became a substitute for alcohol.

My mother's physical decline began at a bar one ill-fated winter afternoon in 1993. While I was ordering her usual hot cappuccino and cream bun, Caitlin lost her balance and fell off the bar stool onto the marble floor. An ambulance took her to the hospital, where I was told she had fractured her pelvis and her right hip-bone. When the doctors showed me her X-rays, for the first time I realized the dreadful decalcification of her bones. A subsequent long period of confinement in bed and then in a wheelchair, along with bad blood circulation, periodic high fever and alarming loss of weight, brought the slow and inexorable deterioration of all her vital organs.

Her last words to me were "I will always love you, Coco." She passed away on August 1, 1994, at the age of eighty-one after twenty years of sobriety.

For me, reading about my mother's life with Dylan is like a nightmare. Had she not achieved complete sobriety, these memoirs would never have been written. The enormous work that has gone into this book is my way of hugging her. Mommy, I will always be proud of you.

Francesco Fazio
Taormina, Villa Paradiso, Sicily, 1997